ELLA AND CHARLES NAPER

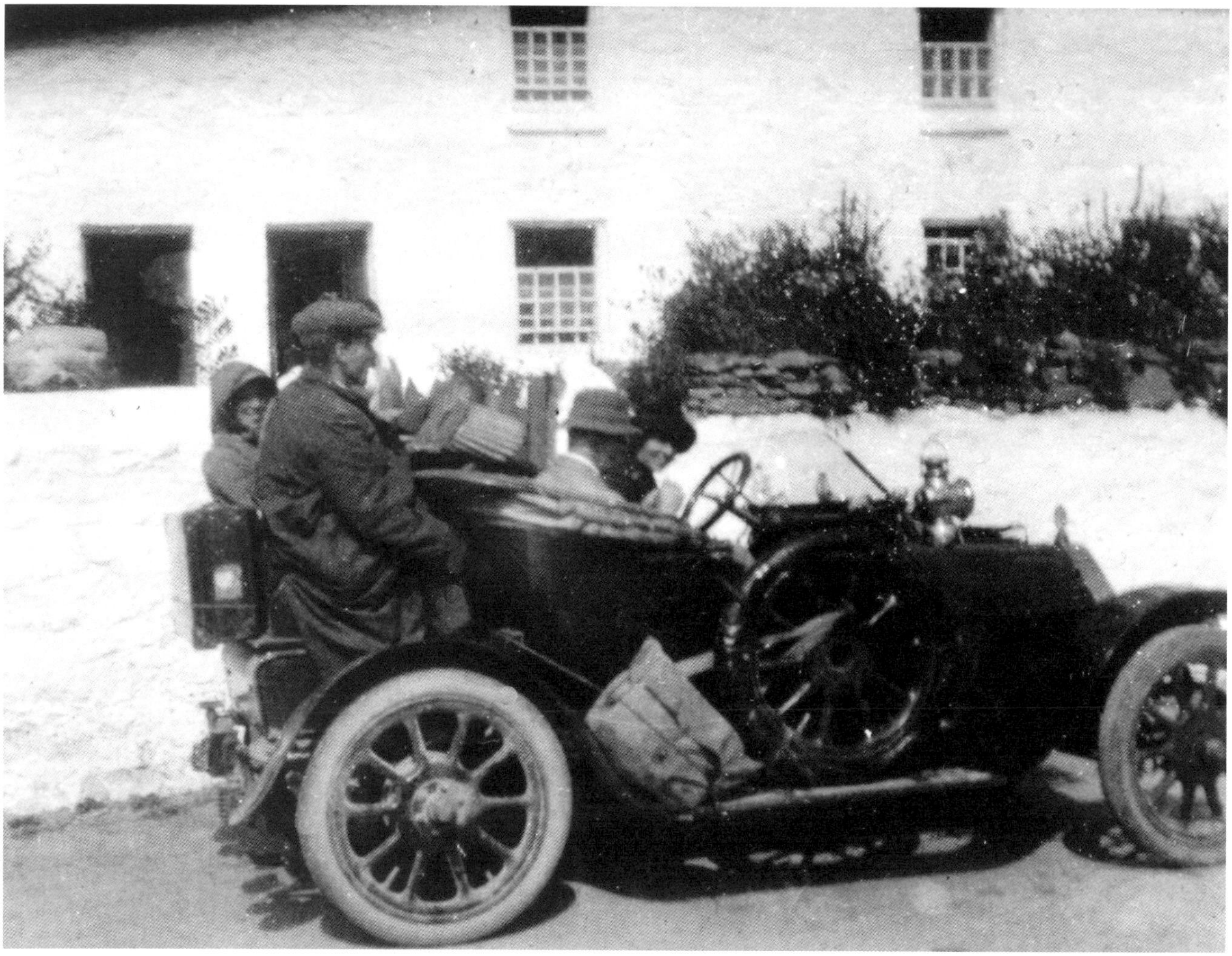

Ella and Charles Naper
Art and Life at Lamorna

JOHN BRANFIELD

Sansom & Company

in association with

PENLEE HOUSE
Gallery & Museum

FRONT COVER
Spring 1916
Laura Knight
Oil on canvas, 60 x 72 in
© Tate, London 2003

FRONTISPIECE
Setting out from Oakhill for Dozmary, 1914

First published in 2003 by Sansom & Company Ltd, 81g Pembroke Road, Bristol BS8 3EA, in association with Penlee House Gallery and Museum, Penzance.

ISBN 1 904537 04 9

British Library cataloguing in Publication Data:
A catalogue record for this book is available from the British Library

Photo credits: With a few exceptions, the colour photographs for this book were taken by Rob Jewell Photography.

Designed and typeset by Gendall Design, Falmouth, Cornwall and printed by HSW Print, Tonypandy, Mid-Glamorgan

Text set in Monotype Sabon 10/16pt.

Contents

All jewellery is by Ella Naper, unless otherwise stated.

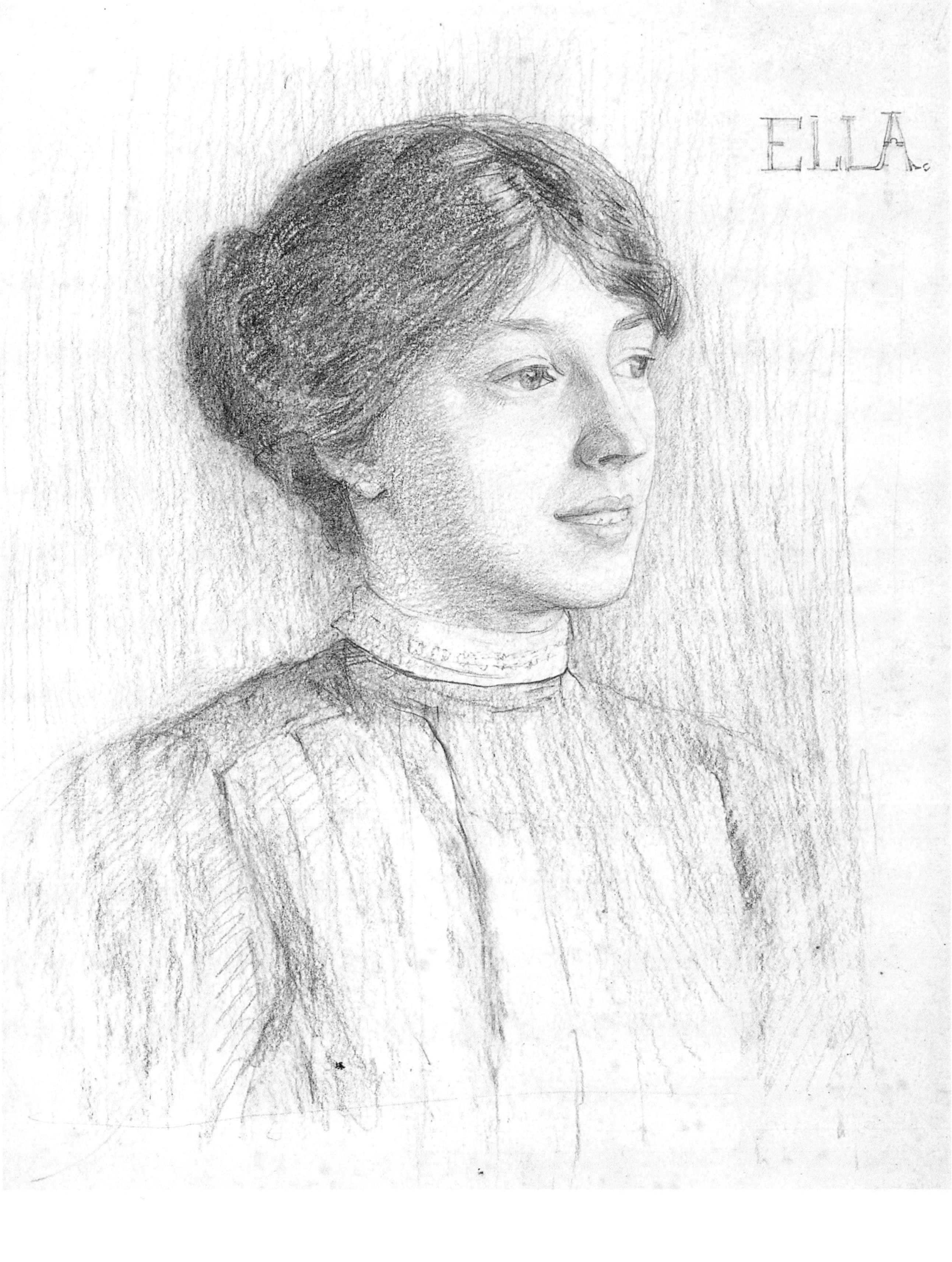
ELLA

Acknowledgements

My main debt of gratitude is to Maryella Pigott, a true keeper of the memory of her aunt and uncle, Ella and Charles Naper. She initiated the writing of this biography and gave me access to their account books and diaries, photograph albums and correspondence, as well as to the special atmosphere of the house and garden that Ella and Charles created, and that Maryella has so beautifully maintained and extended. I am also indebted to her daughter, Sarah Lay, whose project this originally was but whose work and family commitments left her little time.

The archive provided most of my material, but anyone who writes about the Lamorna artists is bound to refer to the seminal study by Austin Wormleighton, *A Painter Laureate: Lamorna Birch and his Circle*, which Sansom & Company published in 1995. Another valuable source was *Laura Knight* by Janet Dunbar, Collins 1975, as was Laura Knight's autobiography, *Oil Paint and Grease Paint*, Nicholson and Watson 1936. I learned about the craft of the silversmith from *Art Nouveau Jewelry in Europe and the United States* by Vivienne Becker, Thames and Hudson 1985. When the publishers reprinted this major study in 1998 they could have illustrated the cover with any of the famous names, Fabergé, Gallé, Lalique; they chose instead the comb in a waterlily design by Ella Naper.

Other books which I found useful were:

Hugh Bedford, *Frank Gascoigne Heath*, published privately 1995

Hazel Berriman, *Arts and Crafts in Newlyn 1890-1930*, Newlyn Art Gallery 1986

Burke's Landed Gentry of Ireland

Ithell Colquhoun, *The Living Stones*, Peter Owen 1957

Melissa Hardie (ed), *100 Years in Newlyn: Diary of a Gallery*, Newlyn Gallery 1995

Kenneth Harris, *Attlee*, Weidenfeld and Nicolson 1982

PAGE 6
Portrait of Ella c.1910
Charles Naper
Pencil drawing

Jim Hosking, *Boskenna and the Paynters*, published privately 1999

Fiona MacCarthy, *William Morris*, Faber and Faber 1994

Nikolaus Pevsner, *The Buildings of England: Devon*, Penguin 1952

Gerald Priestland, *West of the Hayle River*, Wildwood House 1980

Diana Souhami, *Gluck, Her Biography*, Pandora 1988

C.E. Vulliamy, *Unknown Cornwall*, The Bodley Head 1925

Bernard Walke, *Twenty Years at St Hilary*, Methuen 1935

Dorothy Yglesias, *The Cry of a Bird*, William Kimber 1962

Magazines referred to were *The Studio*, 1905, the *L.C.C. Staff Gazette*, 1925, *The Listener*, 1940 and various numbers of *The Flagstaff*, the newsletter of the Lamorna Society. I am grateful to the Curtis Brown Group Ltd., London, on behalf of the estate of Dame Laura Knight, for permission to quote from her autobiography and her letters to Ella, to Adam Kerr for the letters of Lamorna Birch, to the Ullman family for those of Alfred and Cicely Sidgwick and to Meriel Staveley for those of her father, Lenox Naper. Lt-Cdr Peter Staveley sought out information on Charles's schooldays and brother George.

Institutions which were helpful were Camberwell College of Arts; The Cornwall Centre, Redruth; the Cornwall Family History Society, Truro; Greenwich Local History Library; Haileybury College; Penzance Library; the Royal College of Arts; the Royal Navy Submarine Museum, Gosport; the Walker Art Gallery, Liverpool, and the War Graves Commission.

I was glad to speak to people who remembered Ella and Charles: Pat Male, Stella Pakeman, Valerie Powell and Susan Rowe. Sarah Lay recorded interviews with Mary Scobey and Leonora Simpson. Expert descriptions of Ella's jewellery were provided by Barbara Kirk. Further research on the internet was carried out by my daughter Frances and son Peter. Louise Eslick put my manuscript on to disc. I am grateful to all of these, to my wife Pep and son Stephen for practical help, and to John Sansom of Sansom & Company Ltd and the staff at Penlee House Gallery and Museum, Penzance.

Ella: The Art Student

CHAPTER ONE

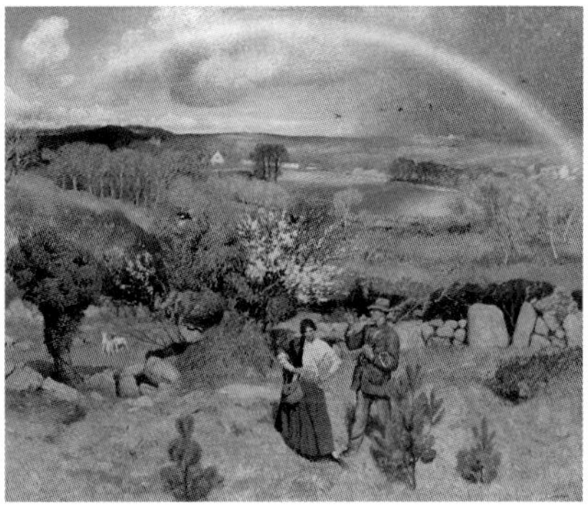

Spring 1916
Laura Knight (see page 50)
Oil on canvas, 60 x 72 in

In 1916 Laura Knight painted her large five foot by six foot canvas *Spring*, now in Tate Britain. It is a beautifully evocative picture of the Cornish countryside, with brown moorlands in the distance shadowed by clouds. The tops of the trees which line the meadows are about to burst into leaf, tinged with pink and orange. The rougher fields in the foreground are divided by banks of granite boulders topped with ivy, yellow gorse and the dazzling white blossom of blackthorn. There are lambs in a field, a ploughman following his horse, swifts flying across the sky. In the front of this scene, bathed in a reddish-gold light, stand a man and a woman. He is tall, wearing the soft hat and deep-pocketed jacket of a fly-fisherman and carrying a rod. She is slender, dark-haired and graceful in a white blouse and long red skirt, a striking black and red shawl over her shoulder. Who are they, this Adam and Eve in the Garden of Eden?

The couple in the foreground are Ella and Charles Naper (pronounced Napper) who lived at Trewoofe (pronounced Trove) at the head of the Lamorna valley. She was a jeweller, he was a painter. Early in the twentieth century they came to Cornwall in search of a way of life which freed them from the conventions of society. They had made a decision to care only about what really mattered to them, the enjoyment of nature, the nurturing of friendships and the creation of beautiful things: a home and garden, jewellery, ceramics and paintings. In the artists' colony at Lamorna they found what they were looking for.

Ella Louise was born on 9 February 1886 at 14 Charlton Terrace in Charlton, south-east London, an area which had developed to house the growing population of Victorian London, the expanding army of city clerks, shop assistants and public service workers. There is something of a mystery about her surname. She was the fourth of nine children, all born in Charlton or Lewisham. They were recorded variously as Couchman,

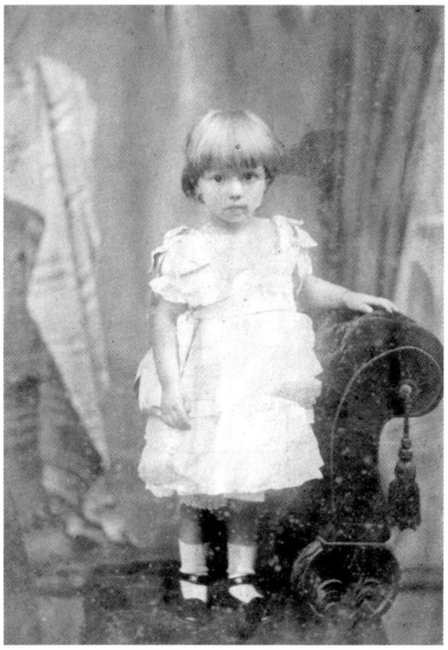

Ella as a child

Couchman-Steele or Steele. Ella's birth certificate has her name as Steele. And yet they were generally known as Champion, the surname that Ella used before her marriage.

The uncertainty goes back to her father Adolphus Steele, who was born in 1859. He was an illegitimate child, and romantic stories circulated in the family about his birth, that his father was an Oxford don or a country landowner who had a child by one of his maids. Whoever his parents were, Adolphus Couchman-Steele chose throughout his life to be known as Alfred Champion.

Alfred married a Lewisham girl, Mary Ann Weeks, when he was twenty-one. He is described on the marriage certificate as a carpenter. He worked for thirty-five years for the London County Council Fire Brigade, rising to the rank of inspector. In his retirement speech he spoke of the happiness and friendship he had enjoyed throughout his official life and the great satisfaction he had derived from his years with the Brigade. The *Staff Gazette* reported that his cheery personality would be missed at headquarters. In private life he was an enthusiastic bowls player and amateur gardener.

Ella's mother was twenty-two when they married and had nine children within eighteen years. As was common in large Victorian families, not all of the children survived. Three died in infancy and Ella grew up with three sisters and two brothers. Her eldest sister Alice, always known in the family as 'Birdie' or 'Chick', had a deformed spine. She grew up to run a secretarial school and lived at home. Her next sister Marion became a domestic science teacher and lived with Hubert Summers-Martin, who taught crafts at Goldsmith's College. They were committed socialists and followers of Keir Hardie. Although they had two children they chose never to marry.

Ella was close to her younger sister Helen (Nell), who was more conventional and in later life was quite satisfied to be a mother and housewife. Like her father, Nell was a keen bowls player, playing at county and international level. She married Henry Male, always known as Jack, who after the First World War went into the city and became senior partner in a stock-broking firm. They were the wealthiest of their generation and lived at Ascot, where they built their home Swinley Edge in seven acres of Berkshire woodland.

Of Ella's two younger brothers, Harry became an engineer for Warner cinemas and Alexander, the youngest in the family and born nine years after Ella, became a successful businessman. He was commissioned in the war and then worked for a London firm of florists and nurserymen. He eventually owned the company and lived next door to his sister Nell in Ascot. He married twice, but had no children.

Apart from their surname, the uncertainty over whether they were Couchman, Steele or Champion, and from Marion's unconventional relationship with Hubert, they were a very average family of the period, affectionate to each other and keeping in touch as they grew up. They would not have stood out in any way in their suburban environment. Their interests were family, bowls, gardening; no one showed any artistic talent or interest in the arts. The exception was Ella. She was the odd one out in her rather Pooterish family. The only photograph of her early years is a portrait taken when she was about three or four. She has dark anxious eyes beneath a fringe of hair and stands with her left hand resting on the back of a chaise longue.

At the age of eighteen in 1904, without leaving the family home, she started a two-year course at the Camberwell School of Arts and Crafts. The School was on a main route out of London into Kent, a red-brick building in a residential area of three-storey terraced houses. It had been founded in 1896 by John Passmore Edwards, the Cornish-born proprietor of a London newspaper who had endowed Newlyn Art Gallery the previous year. It was Ella's first link with Cornwall.

Camberwell was one of the many art schools set up in the second half of the nineteenth century which were run by the local authority, paid for by public money raised through the rates, and placed an emphasis on the practical arts, on courses that could lead to useful careers. The list of classes at Camberwell put modelling, pottery, trade subjects and handicrafts first, followed by drawing and painting. The name echoes the Arts and Crafts movement of the nineteenth century. William Morris in particular believed that individual craftsmanship was being destroyed by mechanisation, that the work produced by machines was soul-less and that the worker in a factory was denied any satisfaction in the finished product. He looked back to the Middle Ages, when craftsmen worked together in guilds to make objects that were practical and decorative, and that gave pleasure to both the maker and the user.

Morris and his followers raised the status of crafts; art was not only oil paintings on the walls of the rich, it was in ordinary everyday objects, in buildings and furniture, in pots and metalwork. Jewellery was not only for the display of valuable gems; inexpensive brooches, buckles and haircombs could be well-made works of art. The Arts and Crafts movement had a vision of society in which art would give personal fulfilment to the creator and bring enjoyment into the lives of ordinary people.

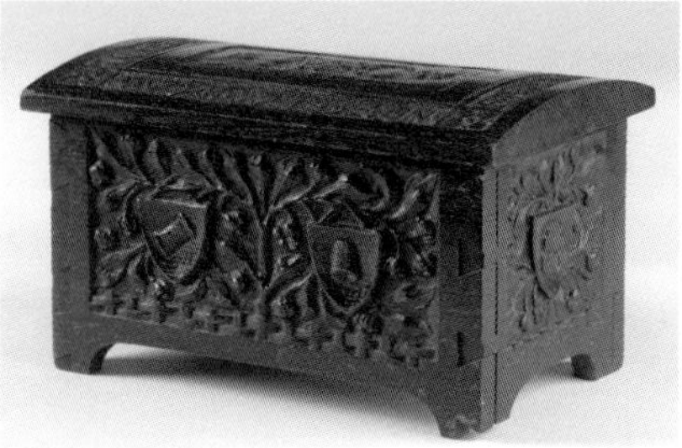

The sewing box Ella made for her sister while at Camberwell, 1905

Ella's work was rooted in these ideals. At Camberwell she learned a wide range of techniques. She studied design and made her own drawings in the studios, carrying them out in the workshops. Enamelling was central to the Arts and Crafts philosophy. It involved a non-precious metal, usually copper; it gave the designer the opportunity for self-expression whilst achieving some striking effects. Ella learned how to prepare copper with a flux on which colourful powdered glass was dusted; it was then fired in a kiln. It required a lot of delicacy and skill to achieve a good result, and even then it often ended in failure. She learned all the variations of basic enamelling, cloisonné, plique à jour, cabochonné and champlevé.

The training was thorough, and Ella practised more than metalwork and enamelling. In her second year she produced a sewing box made of oak, with dovetailed joints and deep carving on all surfaces. It was dedicated to her sister Alice and her initials in solid letters are spread across the centre of the lid with the date: 19 AMC 05. A motto forms a band around the edge, with a rose in each corner: A WORK WELL BEGUN / IS HALF END / ED ILL DONE MUST BE / DONE AGAIN (a sentiment which reflected the ethos of the school). The front panel shows a trailing vine with grapes surrounding two shields on which are carved a cotton reel and a thimble. The two shields on the back depict knitting needles and wool and on the sides, amongst leaves and flowers, are a spool and needles in a sewing case. As a student piece it is impressive in itself, but also in the amount of work and the hours of careful carving that must have gone into its making.

She made a bookplate for herself in her engraving course: EX LIBRIS ELLA L CHAMPION. Beneath a fully-leaved apple tree kneels a very slender Eve, bare-backed and surely a self-portrait. She turns her head to the side and is about to bite into the apple that she holds, with every intention of enjoying it to the full and not caring for the consequences. In front of her sits a monkey, who stares at her adoringly. If the oak sewing-box is the work of a conscientious student, the bookplate is much more self-expressive, a clear image of herself and her expectations for the future. She was by now a beautiful young woman, with dark eyes and long dark hair. A plaster cast was made of her head while she was at art school; she described the horror of being wrapped in wet bandages, with two holes for the nostrils through which to breathe. Her slim body was compared to the *Rokeby Venus*.

The courses being of a practical nature, with the aim of producing craftspeople who could make a living in the world, the students were encouraged to show their work. The Board of Education set up the National Competition of Schools of Art, with gold, silver and bronze medals awarded for work of the highest standard. Ella won at least one national prize, being presented in 1906 with a book on enamelling. It was awarded for success in Subject 24a; the size of the number indicates the variety of work that students undertook.

At Camberwell, she also came into contact with the other influence upon her work, Art Nouveau design. The term dates from 1895, when a gallery of that name opened in Paris to sell modern decorative arts; it brought an exhibition to the Grafton Galleries in London. Emile Gallé, best known for his glass, began to exhibit jewellery at the same time, and Lalique had immensely successful shows at the Grafton Galleries in 1903 and at Agnew's in 1905. Queen Alexandra visited and bought a piece; Calouste Gulbenkian saw the exhibition and ordered one hundred and forty-five pieces. Art Nouveau was all the rage, and Ella embraced it whole-heartedly.

Directly and indirectly, her work was influenced by two English artist-craftsmen. Charles Robert Ashbee was the most influential designer of Arts and Crafts jewellery. A self-taught silversmith, having read history at Cambridge and been articled to the architect G.F. Bodley, he adhered closely to the principles of William Morris. He lived at Toynbee Hall, a philanthropic settlement in London's East End and started the School of Handicraft there in 1887. The following year he founded the Guild of Handicraft, a co-operative of artist-craftsmen. In 1902 the Guild moved with its workshops and guildworkers to Chipping Campden in the Gloucestershire Cotswolds, with the ambitious plan of turning the whole village into a community of craftsmen.

The influence of C.R. Ashbee was passed on to Ella through Frederick James Partridge, born in Barnstaple in north Devon and trained at the Birmingham Municipal School of Art. In 1902 he joined the Guild at Chipping Campden. He was 'perhaps the best jeweller the Guild ever had', according to Alan Crawford in his book on Ashbee, which also describes him as an attractive and talented figure who was dismissed the following year by Ashbee after a flirtation with a female member of the Guild. In 1905 he was back in Barnstaple with the local Guild of Metalworkers and his work was reviewed and illustrated in *The Studio* of that year. He was a particularly skilled worker in horn, a material that exemplifies the Arts and Crafts philosophy of shaping something humble and inexpensive into a work of art. The article is illustrated by photographs of three combs, or ornaments for the hair, made of horn set with cabochon stones in a design based on leaves and fruit. Also illustrated are silver and enamel buckles and a wisteria pendant. This beautiful ornament later belonged to Ella.

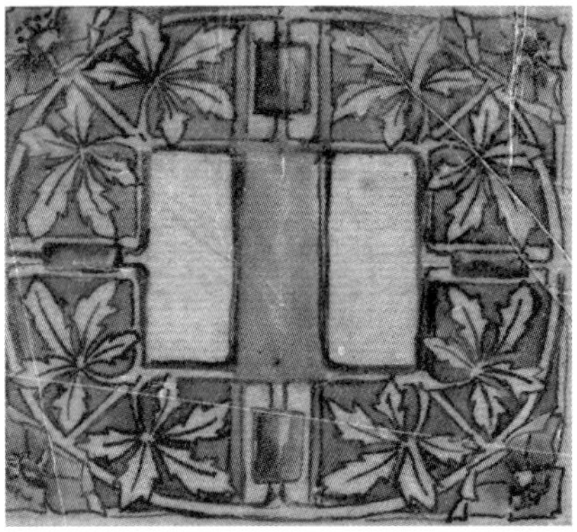

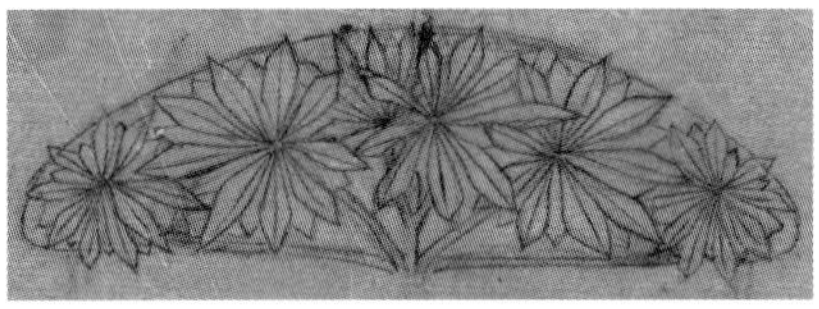

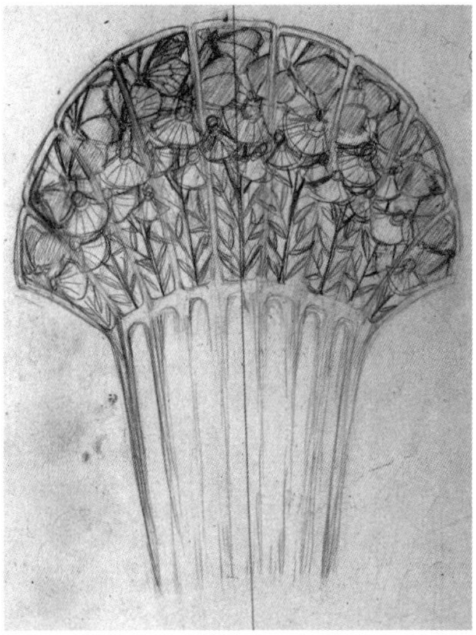

Designs from Ella's sketchbook

After leaving Chipping Campden, Partridge taught at Camberwell. He must have been impressed by Ella's student work for he invited her to join him in Devon as soon as she finished her training in 1906. He had moved to the south coast of the county. Branscombe is a picturesque village just inland from the sea between Sidmouth and Seaton. Here he rented three cottages and established a jewellery workshop. It was run on the lines of the guilds that he had known in Barnstaple and Chipping Campden. It was a co-operative; Ella came to Branscombe not as an assistant or employee, nor as an apprentice or trainee. She worked on her own, on her own pieces of jewellery, but within a group that gave mutual support. There were one or two other workers there, and the wife that Fred had recently married. May Hart was a skilled enameller who had worked for Ashbee on jewellery and silverware. Perhaps she had been the object of Partridge's flirtation at Chipping Campden which had upset Ashbee so much. She too had left to teach at Camberwell.

Ella's early jewellery was very similar in style to Partridge's. Both had an instinctive feeling for natural forms, the organic growth of flowers, fruit, leaves and tendrils, and never stretched the shape into the exaggerated line of some Art Nouveau design. Ella, with a love of plants that was to be expressed later in her garden at Trewoofe, never lost sight of the plant itself. Her starting point was to sketch from nature and her surviving sketchbooks show how she worked, translating her delicate studies into designs.

A Winsor and Newton sketchbook of this period contains drawings of star thistles and tufted vetch, honeysuckle and harebells, fuschia, teazles, ears of corn and clusters of berries, pansies and ivy leaves. There are butterflies and dragonflies. These were then used as the basis for jewellery designs, the drooping fuschias formalised into a hairpiece or tiara and the naturalistic vetch transformed into the repeated pattern of a belt and clasp, with a note 'gilded stems and tendrils, purple leaves'. The designs that were to be used were traced. The faded brown tracing paper is still in place over the elaborate design of butterflies resting on flowers in the nine panels of a comb. It remains because only two of the panels were completed. Other tracings were transferred to the metal or horn on which the design was to be worked. Pages are torn out, half pages cut away to be used elsewhere. Of '80 leaves of good white paper' only thirteen and a half remain.

This is a workbook, and conveys a sense of the jeweller's creative process. It contains a beautiful design on the back of an envelope: two tiny nude figures embrace amongst a cluster of hazel leaves. Later it is simplified into a pendant on a scrap of paper, the figures left out and notes written in

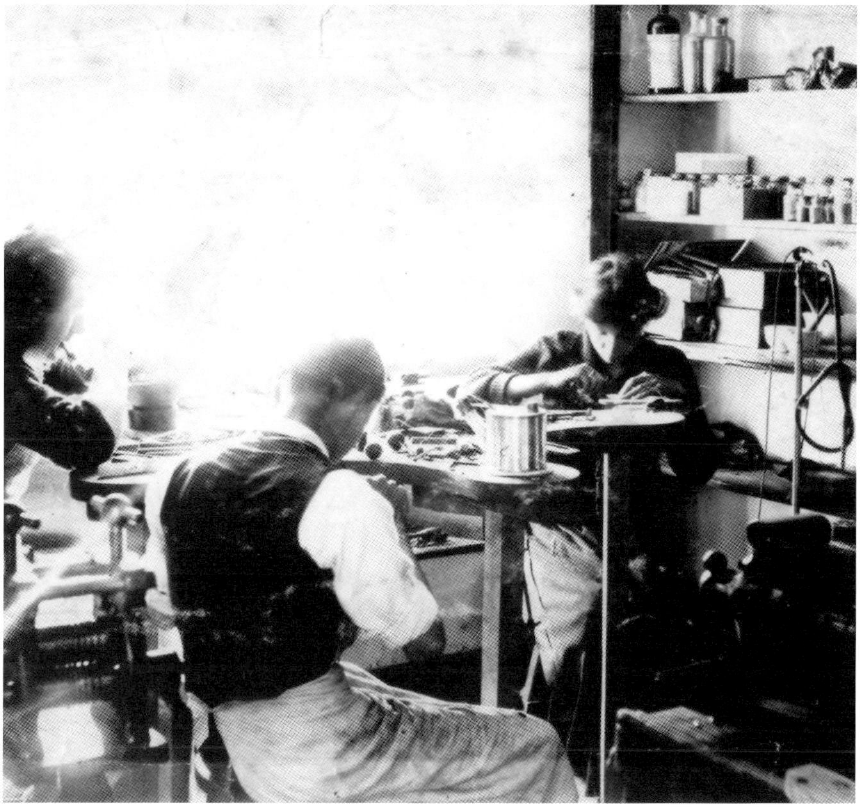

Ella working with Fred Partridge at Branscombe c.1910

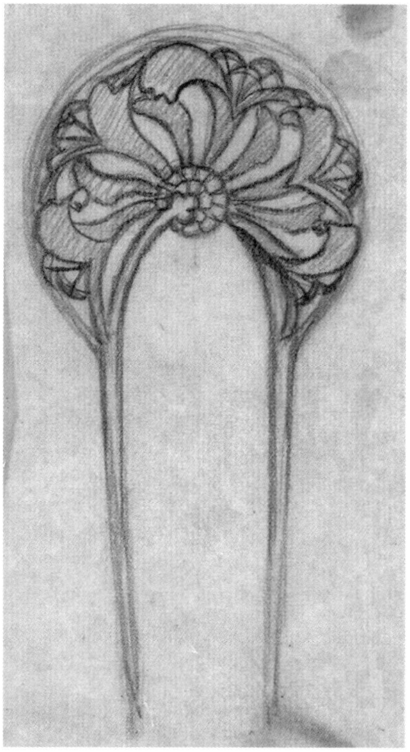

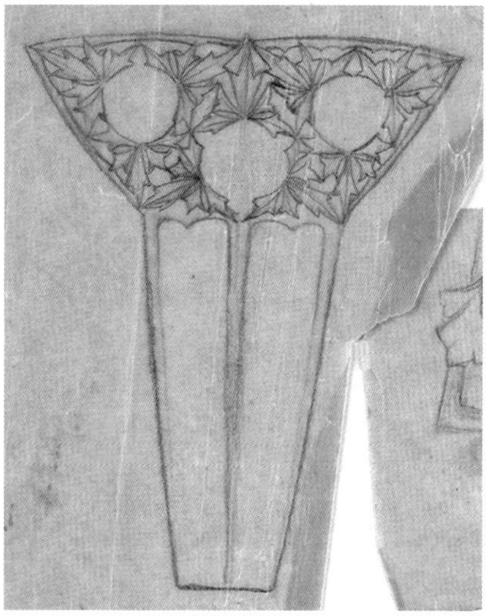

on the materials to be used: pearl, emerald or aquamarine, green enamel.

A photograph taken during her three years at Branscombe shows Ella working at her high jeweller's bench, with Fred Partridge and another at work in the same small room. There are pieces of equipment around them, heavy vices and presses, and shelves with boxes and bottles. Ella is concentrating upon her work, with both hands only a few inches below her face. She conveys a sense of total absorption in what she is doing. In all images of Ella she either adopts a pose for the photographer or artist, or is still and self-contained, completely engaged in a task.

Everything had to be perfect. Fred Partridge was a total perfectionist and the reviewer in *The Studio* wrote: 'It is by no means unusual for him to throw on one side weeks of work, so strong has become his desire to reach perfection of craftsmanship.'

Life at Branscombe was dedicated to work. A hundred miles to the west were students at Stanhope and Elizabeth Forbes' School of Painting, some devoted to their art and some filling in time until they married. There was much more social life in Newlyn: visits to each other's lodgings, concerts and dances, play-readings and parties. Branscombe was a small working community, isolated and intense. There was the company of each other, like-minded individuals with a shared commitment to producing beautiful objects. There was shop-talk and discussion, and Ella always read – she loved poetry. She went sketching in the countryside and took walks through the water meadows to the coast and along the sea-shore.

One summer towards the end of Ella's three years there her brother Alex came to spend a holiday with her. He went fishing and fell into conversation with a man who was also fishing from the beach. The friendly young Alex invited him back to the cottage to meet his sister.

And so Ella Champion met Charles Naper, who besides being a keen amateur fisherman had studied at the Royal Academy Schools.

A photograph of a Branscombe interior shows Ella and Charlie sitting at the table which has a large jug of flowers on it, teapot and teacups of an Arts and Crafts design. They made a handsome couple and they fell in love.

Ella and Charlie at Branscombe c.1910

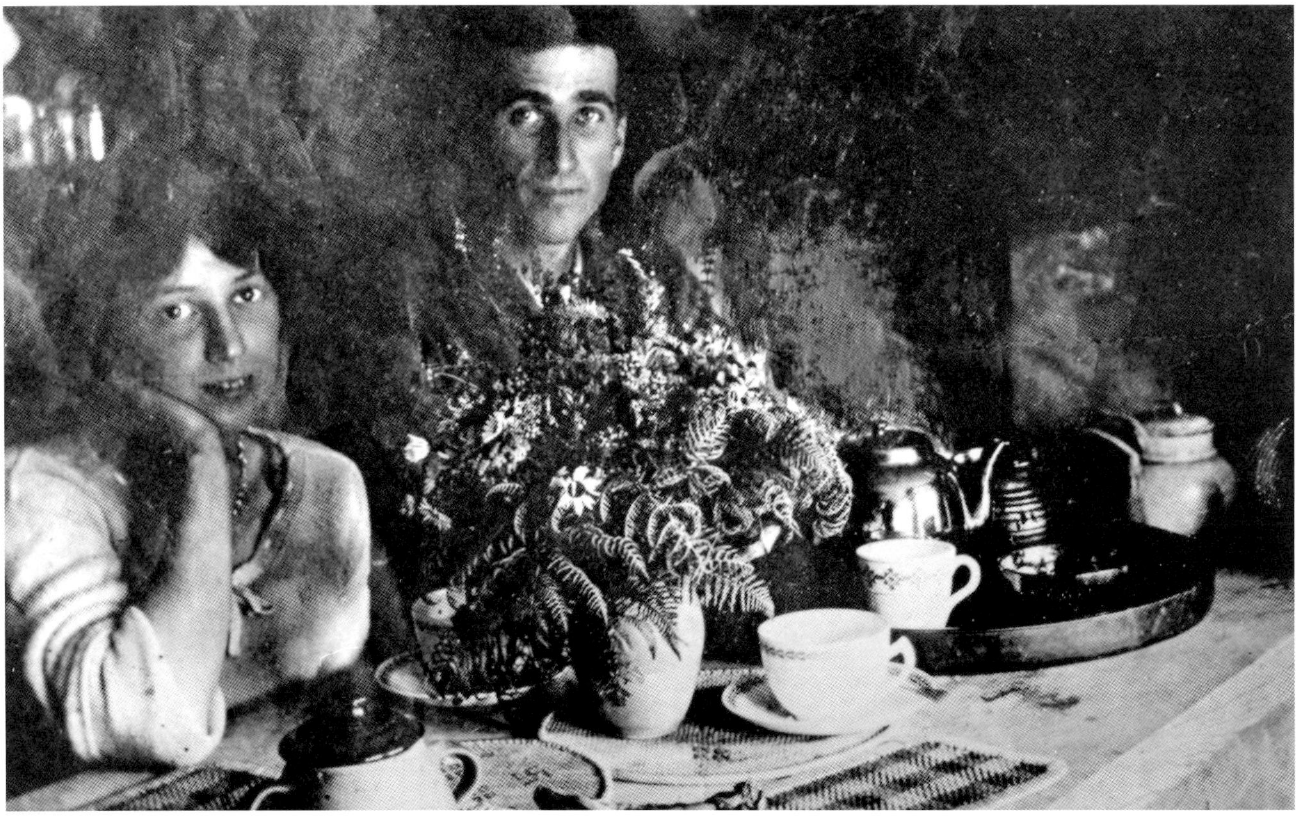

Charles: The Younger Son

CHAPTER TWO

Ella's warm and easy-going family were happy for her. But Charlie came from a very different background. The Napers were an Anglo-Irish family whose connection with Ireland went back to Tudor times. Sir Robert Naper was Queen Elizabeth's Chief Baron of the Exchequer of Ireland. They resided in Dorset, where Sir Nathaniel Naper was a Member of Parliament until the Civil War. When Cromwell recaptured Ireland and rewarded his followers, the Napers acquired the vast estate of Loughcrew, some one hundred and eighty thousand acres in County Meath not far from Dublin.

James Naper became High Sheriff of the county in 1671 and his descendants, always called James or William, followed him in the appointment and made well-connected marriages. Charlie's grandfather James Lenox Naper had the old house pulled down in 1821; he employed Charles Cockerell to build a new Loughcrew House and landscape the garden. The 1830 *Post-Chaise Companion* described it as one of the finest seats in the County of Meath.

James had two sons, James who succeeded him and William who was Charlie's father. William made his career in the army and in 1876 married Jane Wyatt Edgell, who lived with her brother at Cowley House, Brampford Speke, just north of Exeter. It was an elegant, stuccoed late eighteenth-century mansion. After their marriage, Jane moved house several times, their eldest son Lenox being born in Gloucestershire and their next son Frank in London. Their third son Charles William Skipwith Naper was born on 28 October 1882 at Polsloe House, Heavitree, Exeter. Soon after Charlie's birth they moved to Stanley Lodge, Exmouth, and the seaside town remained their home throughout his childhood.

Charles had two younger brothers, George and Edmond, whose twin sister died in infancy. The five boys had the conventional upbringing of their class. After preparatory school, Charles followed Lenox to Haileybury College in

Hertfordshire. Charlie was very shy and he went to Haileybury in the same year as another extremely shy boy, Clement Attlee. The future prime minister described the spartan conditions at the school, the three rows of earth closets, the freezing form rooms opening straight on to the quadrangle, the lack of privacy and the bullying. The food was bad, the teaching uninspired. No one was considered anything unless he was good at games.

Charles left as soon as he was sixteen, having made little impression upon the school. Unlike his brother, he had not joined the Cadet Force; he achieved no mention in the House Records. He was, however, one of the scene painters for the school play. Lenox kept the school informed of every stage of his military career, but the Register has nothing about Charles. Haileybury recorded when he left that he was headed for training as an architect. It was another two years before he entered the Royal Academy Schools and a large architectural drawing survives from this time. It is on paper embossed with the initials R.A. and shows the Garden Front at Hampton Court Palace. It maps every detail of an elaborate façade, including a frieze of sculptured figures. However, in 1903 he abandoned his architecture course and changed to painting, but in Lamorna he was always thought of as an architect. He drew up plans for Duncan's, the house high up towards the coast on the western side of the valley, where the painters Charles and Ruth Simpson once lived. And Trewoofe was to his own design.

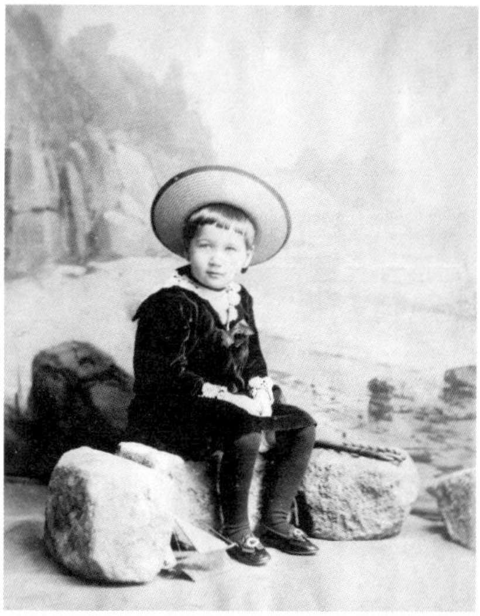

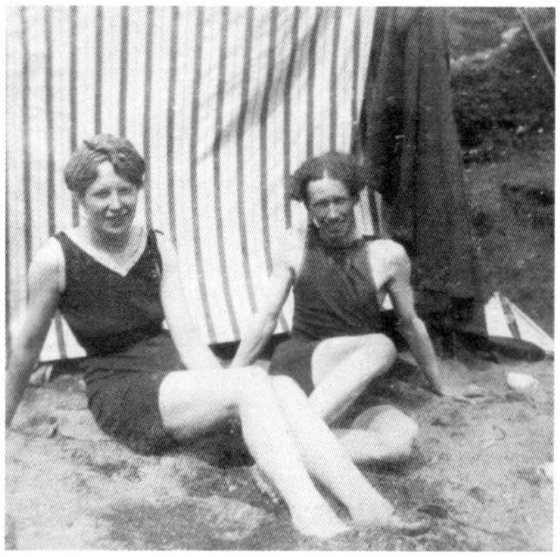

ABOVE
Charlie as a child in Exmouth

Nancy and Hubert Wellington on holiday at Looe c.1912

When he met Ella he was twenty-seven years old. Branscombe was fifteen miles along the coast from Exmouth and Charlie was revisiting the scenes of his childhood. He had not long left the Royal Academy, having spent seven years altogether on his studies. He had not started any work but chose to stay with his mother's family in Devon, painting and fishing, until the day when he followed young Alex Champion up the beach and inland to the cottage at Branscombe.

Having met Ella, whom he adored and worshipped for the rest of his life, he was determined to marry her. For centuries the Napers had married well, uniting with others of property and standing; Lenox was now engaged to Daphne Annesley. Charlie broke completely with tradition. When the wedding took place in the lovely old London church of St Bartholomew the Great in 1910, Lieutenant-colonel and Mrs W.D. Naper did not attend. No wedding photographs have survived, if indeed they were ever taken.

Ella and Charles began a honeymoon at Looe, moving one step closer to the far west of Cornwall; they stayed for two years. They rented a house at Great Tree at the head of a wooded valley leading down to the beach at Millendreath. It was taken for granted in Edwardian England that when a woman married she gave up her work to become a housewife and mother. But Ella was committed to her craft. The jewellery she made at Looe was among her finest work. She had perfected her technique at Branscombe. Now she freed herself from her influences and created original and innovative pieces. The pair of lily-pad combs which feature on the cover of Vivienne Becker's *Art Nouveau Jewelry in Europe and the United States* were probably made at this time. The horn she used is tinted a pale coppery green and the waterdrops which cling to the veined leaves are moonstones of different sizes. They achieve a perfect balance between reality and artifice, and are described by Becker as 'superb'.

The design for a hornwork buckle is based on a circle of oak leaves and acorns. The horn was carved and her carving was – in Vivienne Becker's words – 'skilful, artistic and sensitive'. She devised a technique for overlaying horn with a thin slice of mother-of-pearl to give it a luminous sheen; it required extreme delicacy of workmanship. She continued to work in enamel, being fond of a particularly deep green. She sold her jewellery through the Arts and Crafts Society exhibitions where the guilds regularly showed their work.

Their friend Hubert Wellington, who had studied at the Slade, visited them at Looe. He and his wife Nancy came during the summer and took holiday snaps of them on the beach with their son Bob (who was to become director of the Zwemmer Gallery in London in the thirties), sitting on a seaside donkey. Ella and Charlie also explored the area and discovered Bodmin Moor, only a few miles inland from Looe. They were greatly attracted to its wide open spaces, the empty heathland and vast skies. For Ella this was about as far removed as she could get from the streets of Lewisham, New Cross and Charlton. It must have been at this time that they had the idea of building a hut by the side of Dozmary Pool. The lake was in the centre of the moors, its dark peaty water edged with reeds and surrounded by low hills covered with heather. It was accessible only by track to a primitive farmhouse and the few remains of an ice-works; the ice had been cut out in blocks from the frozen lake in winter and stored in ice-houses ready to be sent down to the fish market in Looe. It had been abandoned in recent years and hardly anyone visited the place.

The hut was like a gypsy caravan without wheels. Fascination with gypsy life was strong at the time; it represented freedom from the stuffiness of Victorian and Edwardian society. Augustus John roamed the lanes of Wales in a vardo, dressed as a gypsy and learning the Romany language. Gypsies and their caravans were painted by Laura Knight and A.J. Munnings.

Charles did an oil painting which shows it in detail. One side was divided through the middle and hinged top and bottom. The lower flap could fold down to extend the floor space into a veranda open to the air and the upper flap was supported on props to extend the roof, rather like a fairground stall. Here they could get away from Looe and were free to be themselves. They could lead a simple life, Charles catching fish in the lake that they would cook on a camp-fire. Ella could dress in workmen's corduroys, play on her mouth-organ, bathe naked in the pool. They were like children playing raggle-taggle gypsies, looking after themselves and living off the land and out-of-doors.

By the standards of the day it was an extraordinary thing to do.

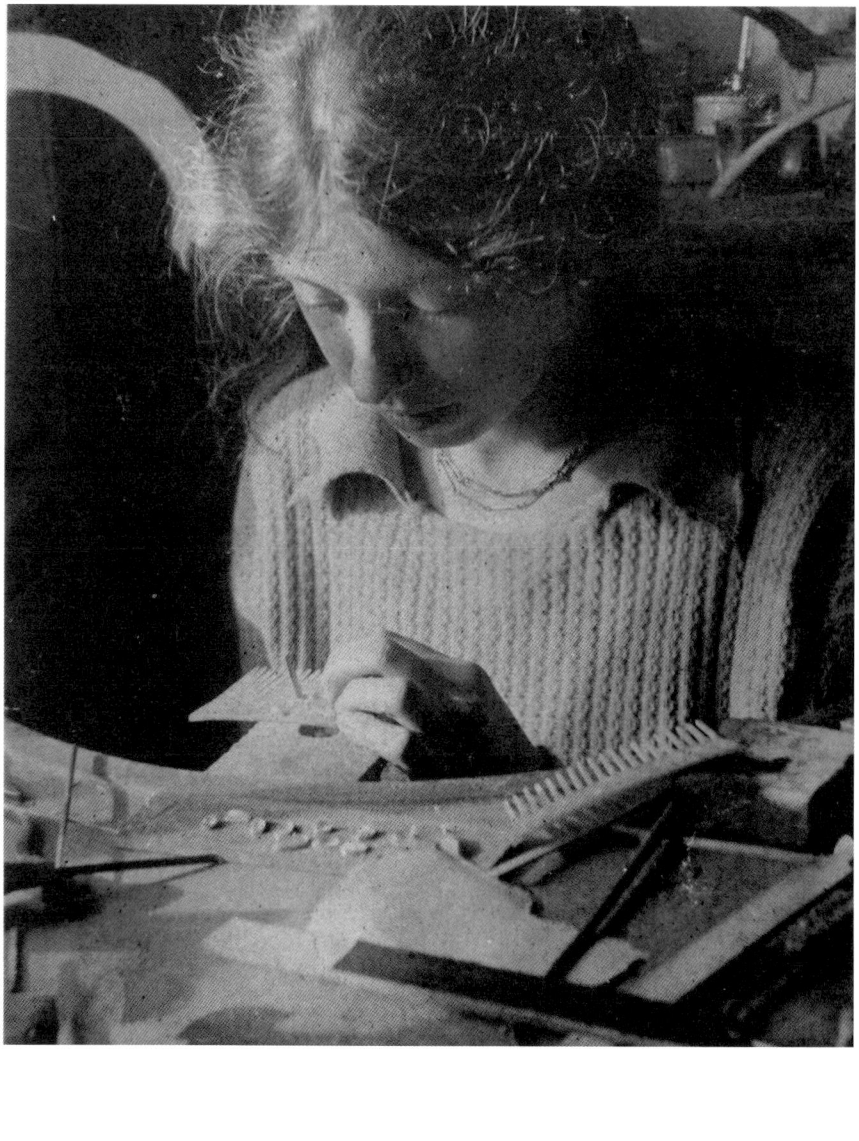

 Ella working at her jeweller's bench

Lamorna Blue

CHAPTER THREE

It was time for them to settle into a permanent home, and they looked further to the south-west. Through her fellow craftsmen in workshops, guilds and exhibition societies, Ella had always been closely in touch with what was going on in the arts. She would have known all about Newlyn and the painters who had settled there since the 1880s. The *plein-air* artists who had flocked in summer to the south coast of Brittany found that there was no need to travel so far, when the fishing village of Newlyn in Mount's Bay on the south coast of Cornwall had as much to offer: a mild climate suitable for painting out-of-doors, picturesque streets, fishermen and their families as subjects and sail lofts as studios. While Ella and Charles were at Looe, Stanhope Forbes in Newlyn was running the painting school with his wife Elizabeth and several of the earliest painters to come to Newlyn were still working there, including Walter Langley, Thomas Cooper Gotch and Norman Garstin. They were well represented each year at the Royal Academy exhibitions.

The visit of Hubert Wellington would have brought them up to date. He was a man with a wide knowledge of the latest developments in the arts world. Recently a number of younger artists had arrived to breathe fresh life into the Newlyn community. Harold and Laura Knight had moved from Staithes in north Yorkshire. Charles Simpson had a studio overlooking the harbour; Ernest Procter and Dod Shaw, soon to marry, were students of Stanhope Forbes. Harold Harvey had grown up in nearby Penzance. At Great Tree and on the beach they would have discussed their plans and if Ella and Charlie had not already thought of moving to west Cornwall it is likely that Wellington suggested and encouraged it.

Ella would also have known of Newlyn as a village with links to the Arts and Crafts movement. Because of the unreliability of the fishing industry, many fishermen were often unemployed. In the belief that a community could be regenerated by handicrafts, J.D. Mackenzie established in 1890 the Newlyn Industrial Class, offering instruction in metalwork, enamelling and embroidery. Two years later John Pearson, the chief metalworker of the Guild of Handicraft joined as an instructor. Their metalwork, especially repoussé copper ware, was put on sale through the exhibition associations. It was natural that Ella and Charles would consider a move towards this part of the county.

But narrow streets and a busy harbour, however picturesque and full of character, were not to their taste. They preferred a quiet valley near the sea, and this was just what Lamorna offered. Samuel John 'Lamorna' Birch had arrived there from Lancashire in 1889, a twenty-year-old self-taught painter. More interested in landscape than figure or narrative painting, he took lodgings at Boleigh Farm at the top of the valley. In 1902 when he married he moved into Flagstaff Cottage, the former harbour manager's house overlooking the cove. By then he had incorporated the name of the valley into his own. The friendly and sociable 'Lamorna' Birch – known as John to his friends – attracted other artists into the area, much in the way that Forbes had done in Newlyn. Alfred Munnings was a frequent visitor, staying at Cliff House, Mrs Jory's temperance hotel. When not painting he could be found at the Wink, the public house on the other side of the road run by Mrs Jory's estranged husband, Nick. Harold and Laura Knight moved out from Newlyn, taking possession of Oakhill at Lamorna Gate. The landowner Colonel Paynter converted the row of cottages into one long house for them. Until it was ready they stayed with the Sidgwicks who had recently built Trewoofe Orchard. Alfred Sidgwick had retired as Professor of Logic at Oxford University and his wife Cecily was a prolific writer of novels with English and German settings and characters, publishing thirty-seven in her lifetime. The artist Benjie Leader and his wife Belle who had lived at Oakhill moved to their new home, Rosemerrin, in the same year.

Two more new houses were added to Lamorna, and some of the more long-standing residents complained that the place was becoming suburban. Robert and Eleanor Hughes built Chyangwheal on the road to Boleigh; they had met as students at the Forbes' School of Painting and had married in St Buryan church in 1910. Frank and Jessica Heath built Menwinnion, the grandest of the houses at the top of the valley. Frank Heath had trained at South Kensington Art School, at Croydon and Westminster; Jessica had been another student of Stanhope Forbes. Lamorna had become a community of artists and writers and the word 'colony' was first used in reference to it in a letter of Birch's of 1912.

It was at this time that Ella and Charles came looking for a house or a plot where they could build. They would have arrived by train at Penzance station and travelled on by motor or pony and jingle along the seafront whose gleaming wet promenade featured in Norman Garstin's *The Rain It Raineth Every Day*. It was a mile to the muddy streets and fish smell of Newlyn, and then came the steep climb up Paul Hill, a rise of five hundred feet in half a mile. As they neared the top they could look back on the harbour filled with fishing boats like tiny models and the whole bay stretching away to St Michael's Mount in the distance. They passed Wheal Betsy, the new house that Gotch had built, and the entrance to Higher Faugan, the home of Stanhope and Elizabeth Forbes, and continued through open country between hedges of windswept trees. On the left was a glimpse of the tower of Paul church, a narrow line of sea beyond it. The road began to drop into a valley and they entered Trevelloe wood. At the bottom were the milk factory and Clapper Mill on the Lamorna stream. A rutted track led into the valley itself, wooded and with occasional houses but with no sight of the sea, only the stream rushing noisily over boulders. Beyond the entrance to Flagstaff Cottage the sea was suddenly before them, the granite quay with its arm across the cove and steep cliffs on either side.

To build a house in Lamorna meant negotiations with Colonel Paynter. The western side of the valley belonged to the Boskenna estate, which he had inherited at the beginning of the century. He was an eccentric character, keen to modernise his scattered and ramshackle estate but not an easy man to deal with. Fortunately, part of his eccentricity was a liking for artists, whom he thought brought colour and style to a backward community, and he was happy to fix them up with accommodation and studios. But he was capable of attaching odd conditions to a lease, insisting that a tenant should have served in the army, played bridge or was not a Roman Catholic.

With the help of Paynter's more reasonable land agent Gilbert Evans, Charles and Ella were able to buy three fields. They were at the very top of the valley and approached by a short track a little beyond Clapper Mill and Oakhill Cottage, just before the turning down into the cove. It led to Trewoofe Manor, the oldest house in Lamorna, though only part of it remained standing, the east wing of the Elizabethan E-shaped building. The granite pillars of the massive central door were still in place, but as an archway in the garden. Trewoofe Farm, its barns and piggeries had been built with the stones from the rest of the ruin. An earlier house had been occupied by a family called Levelis (pronounced to rhyme with 'trellis') since Norman times; a monument in St Buryan church records the death without

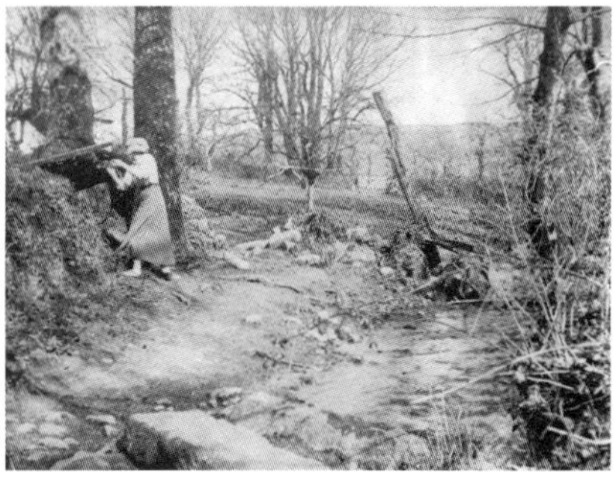

ABOVE
Starting work on the garden

BELOW
An early photograph of Trewoofe

heirs of Arthur Levelis in 1671. They had married into another Norman family, the Trove de Troves. With the passing of time the name had translated into Cornish as Trewoofe, and then with the decline of Cornish had reverted to the Anglo-French 'Trove' in sound though keeping the Cornish spelling.

The cost of the land to Charlie and Ella was two hundred and fifty pounds. Charles went to his family for the money, getting an advance of two hundred pounds in February 1913 against his eventual inheritance from his mother's estate. More railway stocks and shares were sold in September and October releasing a further two hundred and eighty pounds to pay for the building of the house. The previous year Menwinnion had cost one thousand pounds to build, paid for by Jessica Heath's father. Trewoofe House would have to be more of a cottage.

Their three fields lay beneath the brow of the hill and were surrounded by stone hedges. There were sycamore and elm trees around the outer boundaries, the remains of an orchard in the lower field. It was in the top corner that Charlie chose to build their house. From here it was high enough to enjoy the last of the sun in the evening and the best of the view over the rooftops of Trewoofe Manor and the farm towards the side of the valley beyond. Just below was Oakhill, where the Knights became their near neighbours and closest friends.

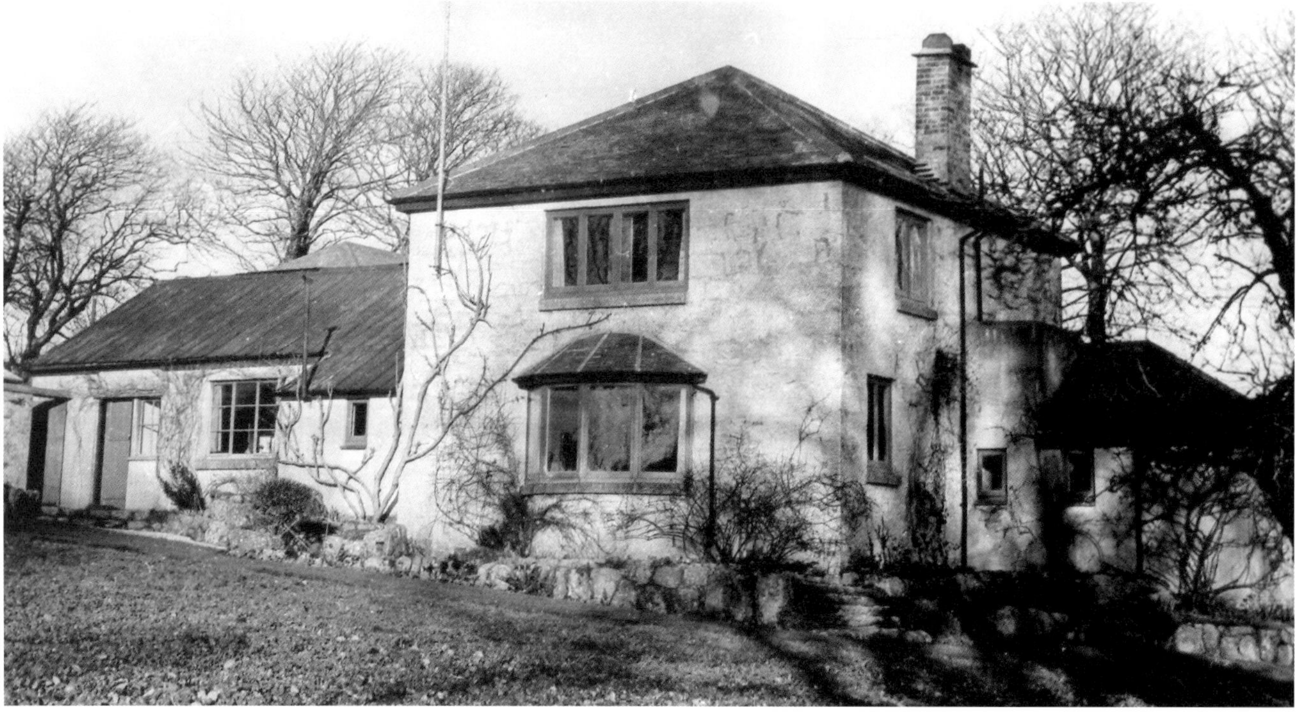

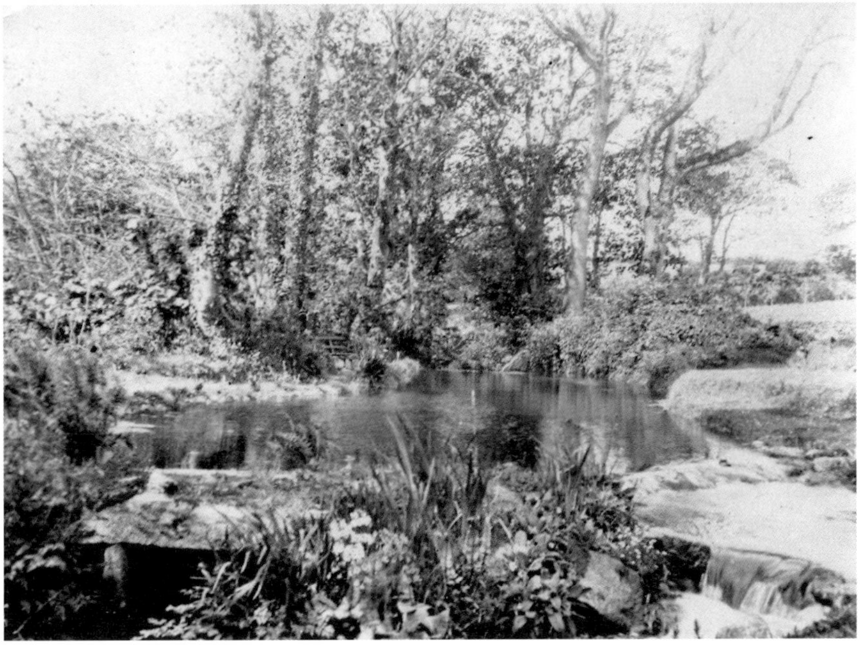

The pond that Charlie made in the garden

The house that Charlie designed was quite simple, a two-storey cube beneath a roof with a single peak in the centre. It was built of stone and slate. Beneath the roof were two bedrooms on the first floor, a kitchen and sitting-room with a bow-window on the ground floor. The one fanciful touch was the bow, which is not traditional in Cornwall but Charlie would have remembered the two full-height bow-windows that were the principal feature of Cowley House. Single-storey buildings projected on either side of Charlie's house, the one to the south on a lower level containing toilet, storerooms and coal-house, the extension to the north providing a bathroom and a workshop for Ella. It led to a large studio for Charles, built at right-angles to the house, with high windows in the north wall.

The kitchen had a coal-fired stove; rain water was collected in tanks behind the studio. Inside it was furnished very simply. Ella painted the window frames and some of the furniture a pale cream, the doors she painted Lamorna blue, a shade between cobalt and Prussian blue. Other furniture she painted the same deep blue and it appeared in bands on the crockery she used, the blue and white Cornishware.

They worked together to create the garden. A leat flowed through the fields dividing them into an upper and lower garden. The water came from a spring some distance away beyond Grambla Barn, passed around a spur of land into Trewoofe Farm and crossed through the Napers' before feeding the pond for Clapper Mill. According to legend it is haunted by the ghosts of

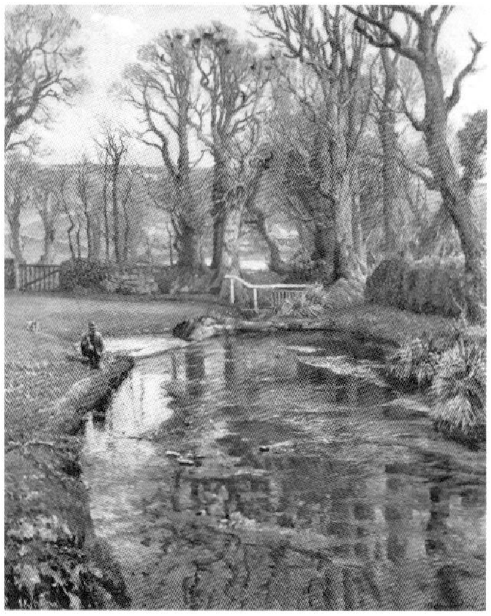

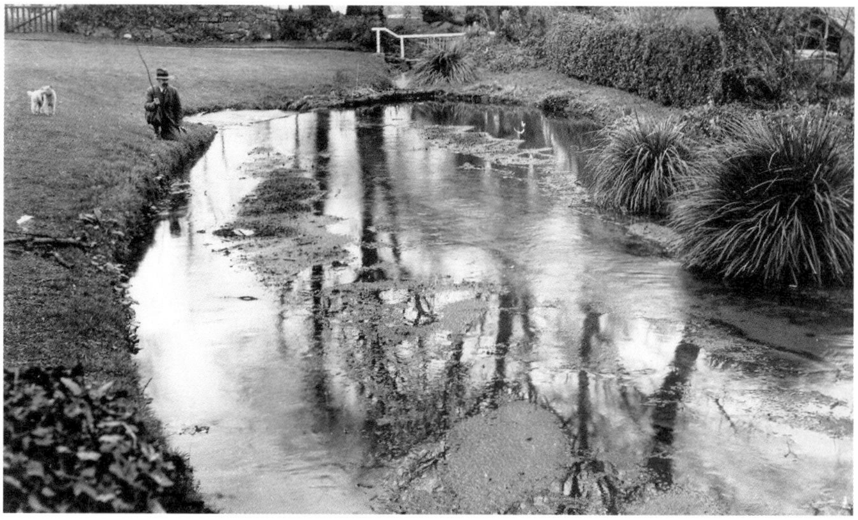

ABOVE
Ella's Garden 1938
Lamorna Birch
Oil on canvas, 47 x 38 in

Photograph of Lamorna Birch and his dog on which Birch based ***Ella's Garden***

two children. Sir Levelis of Trewoofe Manor had gone to the Crusades, leaving his young and pretty wife with two small infants. He was away so long that she gave him up for dead and agreed to marry his uncle, Hugh Levelis. On the day of the wedding her Lord returned unannounced and asked where his children were. Neglected by their mother and her servants they had been gathering flowers by the side of the leat, fallen in and drowned. The two wraiths can be seen floating over the water.

The leat easily became blocked, especially in autumn, but as it was needed by both farm and mill it was always kept open. Charlie dug out a pond that it could feed before flowing on to the mill. He removed one of the Cornish hedges and used the largest boulders to shape the sides. With the other blocks of granite he formed flower beds and steps around the house and a rockery before the front door. He made a sluice gate so that the pond could build up a head of water two feet deep, enough to keep trout in. It needed a lot of maintenance as it quickly silted up, and in later years Charlie spent many hours clearing the leat and digging out the pond.

Working in the garden they were aware of the quiet around them, the peace of the valley emphasised by the natural sounds, the rooks in the top of the elms, the cockerel and hens in the farmyard, the flow of water through the leat. Sometimes, if the wind was in the east they could hear the bells of Paul church and on a foggy night the distant boom of the horn on the Longships.

Like the other two couples who built houses and made gardens at the head of the Lamorna valley at the same time – the Heaths at Menwinnion and the Hughes at Chyangwheal – they had found contentment in a loosely connected artistic community. They all remained for the rest of their lives.

Emerald and Gold: Dozmary Pool

CHAPTER FOUR

Ella and Charles had kept the hut at Dozmary Pool and, although there was work to be done in the garden and on the leat and the pond, they returned there for holidays. When they could bathe in the sea at Lamorna, have picnics on the cliffs and walk the coastal path to Penberth and beyond, it might seem strange to choose to swim in the black peaty water of the lake and camp out by its sedgy margins. Unlike Harold and Laura Knight who spent some months in London every year, Ella and Charles were not looking for city contrasts and never tired of either Lamorna or Dozmary.

The pool, about a quarter of a mile across and a mile in circumference, lies between two gently curving folds of moorland, falling away to the east towards the valley of the river Fowey. The water reflects the form of the moor and the clouds in the sky; everything is reduced to the most basic elements, which give it an austere beauty. It has a sense of a much more ancient past, of prehistoric times and early Neolithic and Bronze Age settlements. It has always attracted myths: King Arthur's last battle was fought on the moors nearby and when Sir Bedivere at the request of the dying King throws Arthur's sword Excalibur out over the water, a hand rises from the lake to grasp it by the hilt and descend back into the depths. The unjust steward Tregeagle was condemned for eternity to empty Dozmary with a limpet shell. If the mist hangs for long over these highest grounds of Cornwall it can seem a melancholy place. In *Unknown Cornwall* C.E. Vulliamy thought it was most wonderful on a still clear night. 'Away to the south-east, across the stern black line of the moors, you see the dim, rhythmic wheeling of a fan of light: that light comes from the great lantern at the Lizard, down on the edge of the sea, some fifty miles off.'

It was only partly the place; it was as much the attitude that Ella and Charles brought to it, a romantic delight in the freedom of its open spaces, its remoteness from conventional society, their wish to share it with their friends.

Their holiday of 1914 has become something of a legend itself in the life-stories of those artists who joined them: Harold and Laura Knight, Harold and Gertrude Harvey. It was a last idyllic fling in the golden days before the First World War until it was all shattered by the guns of the western front.

But the tranquillity of Lamorna had already been broken before the outbreak of war by a domestic tragedy. 'Suddenly the death of a much-loved member of our colony put an end to all joy…' wrote Laura Knight in her autobiography *Oil Paint and Grease Paint*. She was referring to the suicide of Alfred Munning's wife. Florence Carter-Wood had met Munnings when she and her brother Joey were both students of Forbes at Newlyn. Their friends had misgivings about the marriage; 'Blote', as they cruelly nicknamed her because she seemed as cold and remote as a bloater, was beautiful and given to depression, whilst Alfred was extrovert and not particularly sensitive to the feelings of others. On their honeymoon in London she had made her first attempt to take her life. At Lamorna Colonel Paynter's land agent Gilbert Evans gave her sympathy and understanding and they became lovers. Evans was recalled to his regiment and left for Nigeria in April 1914, meeting Florence one last time in London before sailing. On 23 July there was a fancy dress party at Trewarveneth, the farmhouse at the top of Paul Hill that had been the home of the Forbeses, the Gotches, the Knights and currently of Jill and Geoffrey Garnier. Florence left early after A.J. had shouted abuse at her; he had called her a whore, believing that she was pregnant by Evans. After breakfast the next morning she went to their bedroom at Cliff House and again took cyanide; she died shortly afterwards.

Laura Knight was required to give evidence at the inquest. When she returned to Oakhill she found their Belsize car drawn up at the gate. 'On the running boards, mattresses and bedding were rolled and roped, kettles, saucepans and frying pans hung all round; in the dickey-seat sat Charles Naper, wrapped round with an old red eiderdown. All was ready for the journey to Dozmare [sic] Pool on the Bodmin Moors.' They wanted to escape from the Lamorna valley which was no longer a happy place and seek solace in the emptiness of the moor.

Ella was extremely practical, used to handling machines and metals. Laura was impressed by the way she organised the provisions. 'We stopped at Truro to buy stores. Ella Naper knew exactly what we should need. It was the first time in my life that I had done any serious household shopping. It seemed miraculous that anyone should know exactly how much rice, tea, flour and sugar would be required for a month – even matches were not forgotten. In a shop there I found a blazer striped like the rainbow, which

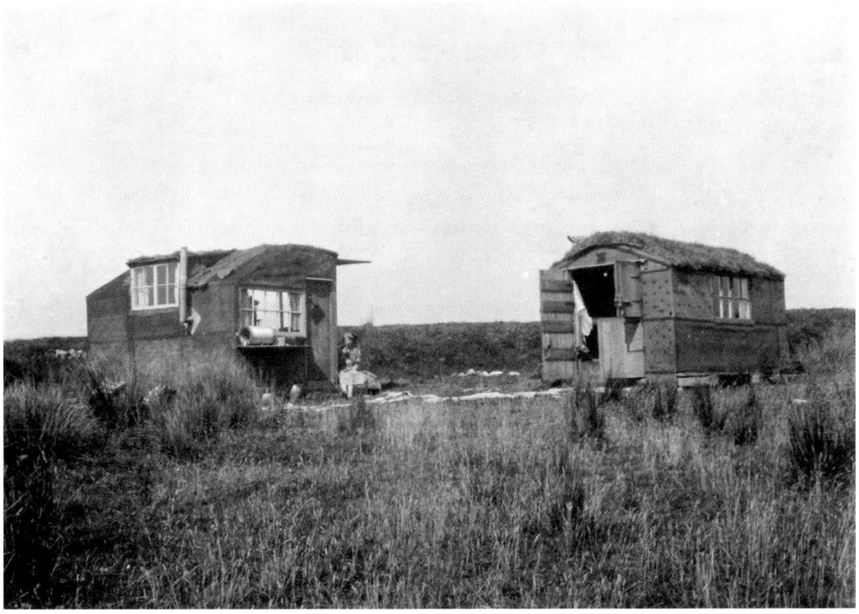

The artists' huts at Dozmary

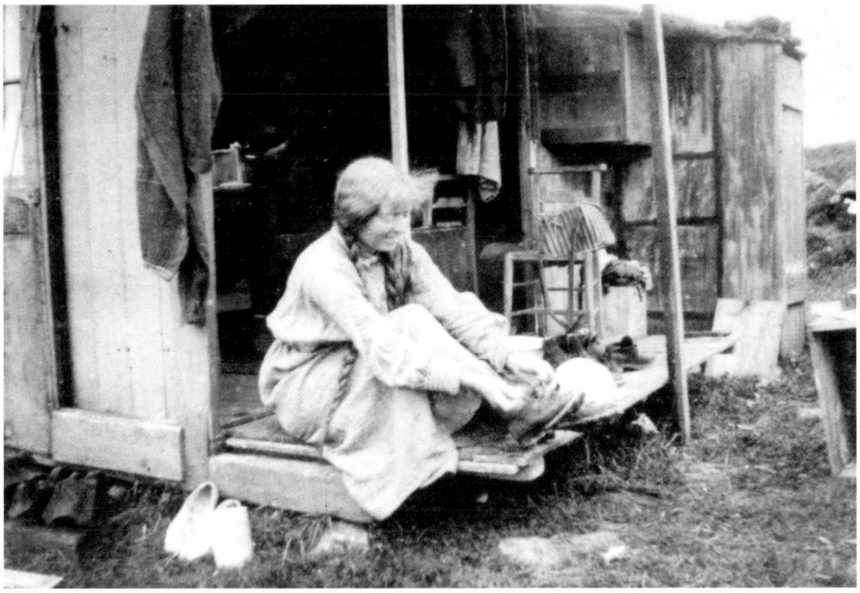

BELOW
Laura Knight at Dozmary

Gert Harvey christened my suit of mourning, for although I bought the gay thing, I could not stop weeping.'

When they got to Dozmary the moor was glorious, the unbroken lines of the hills reflected in the pool, the freshness of the air, the stillness of the water. 'We lived in a little hut that Charlie had built. The Napers' bed stretched across the whole of one end. Harold and I slept in a low tent outside, till it was blown away in a gale one night. Gert and Harold Harvey slept at the farm close by, where they burnt nothing but peat in the open fire, that flavoured deliciously our home-made bread and scalded cream. When

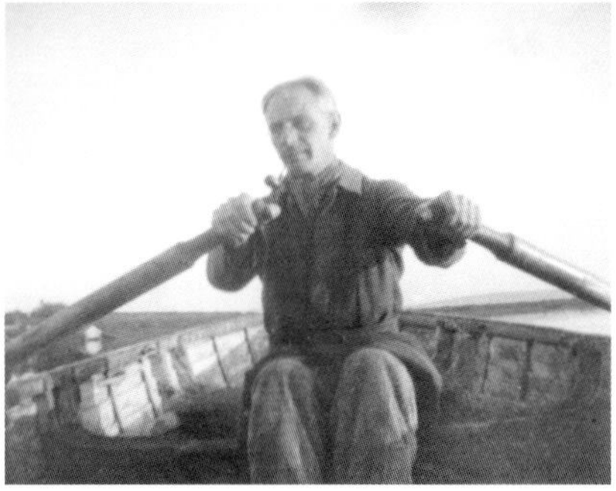

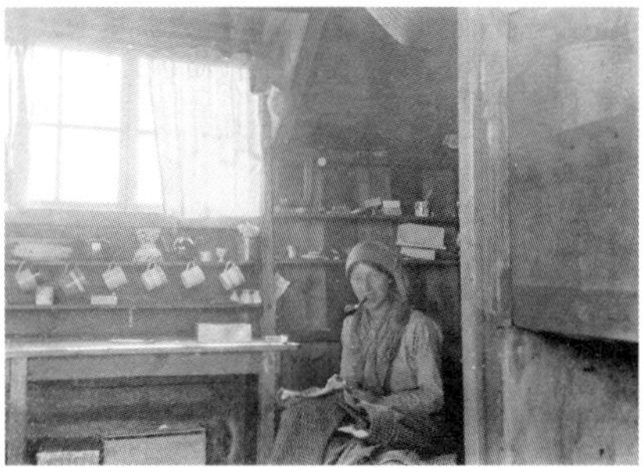

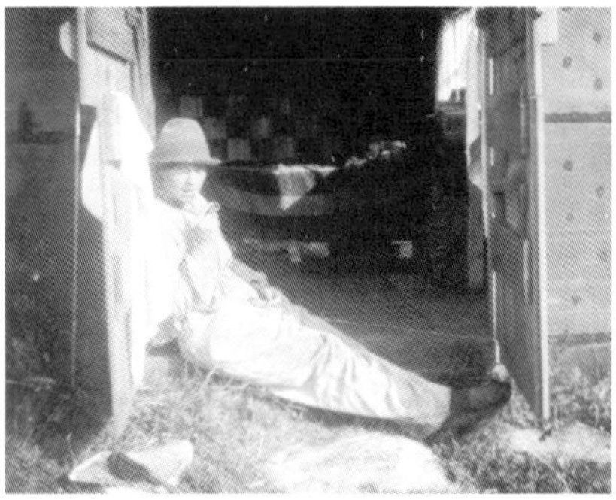

TOP
Harold Knight rowing on Dozmary Pool

MIDDLE
Ella inside the Napers' hut

BOTTOM
Ella relaxing at Dozmary

OPPOSITE
Charlie with Gertrude Harvey

we all crowded into Charlie's hut for meals, not a single other body could have been prised in. The girls did all the housework, the men carted the water for washing the crocks, and we all bathed in Dozmare [sic] Pool.'

But even in the remoteness of Bodmin Moor they could not escape entirely the outside world. Laura was not yet a celebrity, but four visitors in their smartest clothes came seeking her out. She had signed her name in the visitors' book at Jamaica Inn. They caught her when she and Ella were doing the family washing. 'The hut was completely filled with steam and wet linen. Ella, an adorably lovely slim creature, brown as a berry, was dressed in a pair of French workman's corduroy trousers belonging to Harold, her arms bare and covered with suds as she rubbed the clothes in an old tin bath, clay-pipe in her mouth.'

They worked at their painting and sketches and all the chores of the simple life. They tramped miles over the moorland. 'One hot afternoon Gert, Ella and I found ourselves in a wood where Pan might have lived... [a] thick carpet of emerald moss and bright red pine needles – the sumptuously marked grass snake slithering through to drop over the bank into the River Fowey, a mere stream that ran between densely packed pine trees, their trunks mast-like before overhead their branches spread and made a ceiling. Here and there a spindly beech festooned its leaves of palest green over the density of an ink-black pool, gold-spotted where the sun pierced some little hole in the fir branches overhead, turning the peat-stained clear brown water into little patches of pure gold.

'We stripped and went into the pool naked. I shall never forget seeing my two companions in such a setting, one blonde, pearly of skin, the other dusky with long straight black hair.' This picture of Ella, Gert and Laura like water nymphs or naiads sporting naked in the dappled light of a pool on the River Fowey seems like an idyll of innocence in the last few days before the world changed for ever.

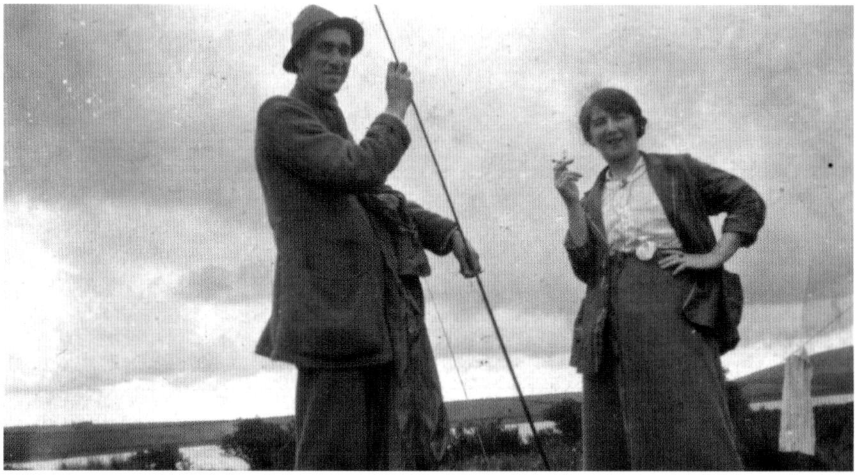

The Great War

CHAPTER FIVE

In the month spent at Ella and Charlie's hut by Dozmary Pool they had no news of the outside world. Towards the end of their stay they went to Plymouth for the day and crossing the ferry at Torpoint they overheard a remark: 'If Russia chips in, France chips in. If France chips in, we chip in!' They realised that the country was on the brink of war. 'Suddenly everything turned black', and their personal tragedy became a national one.

The war made little difference in Lamorna at first. It seemed remote and the drinkers at the Wink even declared their neutrality. But by the spring of 1915, with news of heavy casualties at the front, attitudes had hardened. It was not a good time for artists to sell their work and even producing it became difficult with the restrictions on painting out-of-doors. At first, an almost hysterical atmosphere of suspicion prevailed; on one occasion, Laura Knight was painting children in the harbour at St Ives and dabbed in two spots of paint for the skyline. She was immediately approached and asked to explain what they meant.

Ella suffered less than the *plein-air* painters, working at home in her studio. She was making jewelled frames, for photographs rather than pictures, for an exhibition at the Fine Art Society in London in June 1915, with paintings by Lamorna Birch and Laura Knight. The mood of the show was meant to be sunny, to counteract gloom about the war, and Ella's jewellery sparkled. But they were all affected by a diminishing market and falling prices. Birch was furious when he heard that Charles Simpson had let two hundred paintings go for £100; before long he was accepting big reductions on his own pictures. Harold and Laura Knight had to sell their car.

The first of the Lamorna artists to join up early in 1915 were Frank Heath, Benjie Leader and Joey Carter-Wood. Lamorna Birch and Robert Hughes were in their forties and too old for active service. They joined the local volunteer force and Birch, erect and dapper in full military uniform,

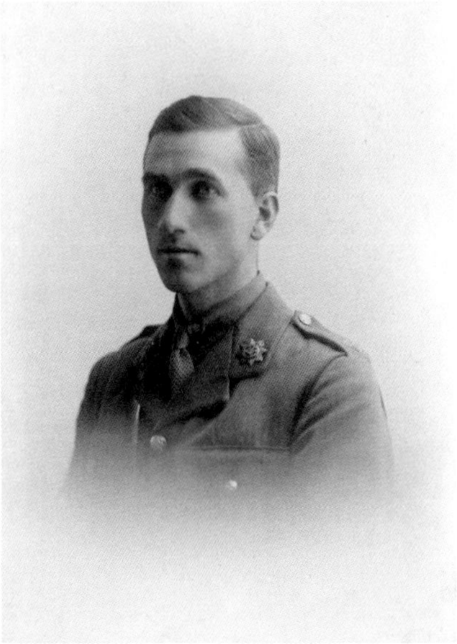

ABOVE
Charlie in the Great War

OPPOSITE
Nanjizal: Towards Land's End
Charles Naper
Oil on board 30 x 40 in

BELOW
Nanjizal: Towards Porthcurno
Charles Naper
Oil on canvas 32 x 40 in

with puttees and highly polished boots, helped to guard Newlyn harbour. Alfred Munnings trained army horses near Reading and then went to France as an official war artist. Ernest Procter joined the Friends' Ambulance unit. Charles Simpson's earlier riding accident prevented him from serving in the army.

Frank Heath was posted to France and almost immediately suffered the effects of a gas attack. After being in hospital in France and London, he was invalided out of the army and returned to Menwinnion to convalesce. Stanhope Forbes's only son Alec died on active service in France in 1915 and Benjie Leader was killed the following year, leaving his wife Belle with two small children. He was the son of the distinguished Victorian painter Benjamin Leader and the family commissioned from Ella the memorial in St Buryan church.

In 1916 Laura Knight painted *Spring*, showing Ella and Charlie setting out for a day's fishing with a wide view of the Cornish countryside beyond them. Laura described the wartime conditions under which it was painted, crouching behind gorse bushes and sketching on a slip of paper so that she would not be seen. When she had drawn a shape she would rush back to the studio to build up the picture from these notes. It was a wartime picture, expressing the newness of spring which always returns; there is a rainbow in the sky. But it transcends its message, and although Charlie and Ella are not convincingly going anywhere or doing anything other than posing, it captures the freshness of spring and the idyllic quality of their life in Cornwall.

It would seem from this picture that life went on much the same for Ella and Charlie during the war. But by the spring of that year Charlie had already been called up for military service and he was painted either from memory or earlier sketches. Later he was painted out, an act without any symbolic significance, and replaced by a boy with a dog, a version reproduced in the Frost and Reed print. After the war it was exhibited in Pittsburgh and returned in a damaged condition. Laura had to repaint sections and at the same time restored Charlie to his position alongside Ella.

Ella did not want to stay on her own at Trewoofe and returned to her family, doing her bit for the war effort by working in the munitions factory at Woolwich. In April Charlie's brother George died on patrol at sea. Early in his career he had joined the submarine branch of the navy and was promoted to Lieutenant-commander just before the outbreak of war.

His death helped to bring the family closer together, a reconciliation that had begun earlier. When so many women were losing husbands and sons,

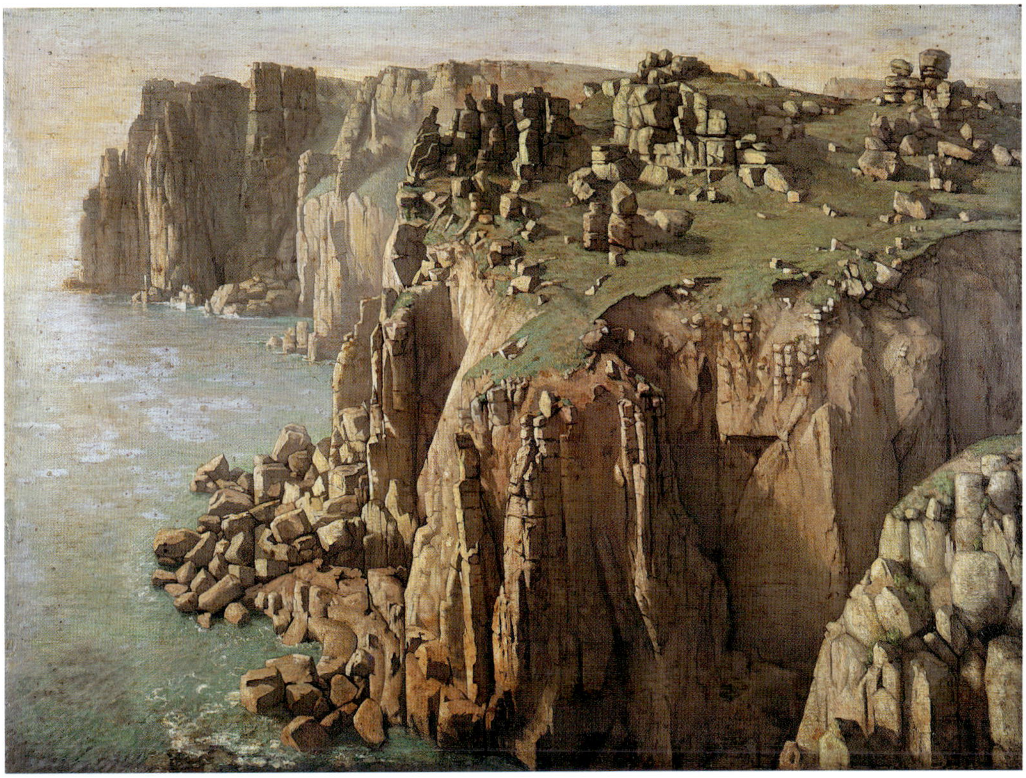

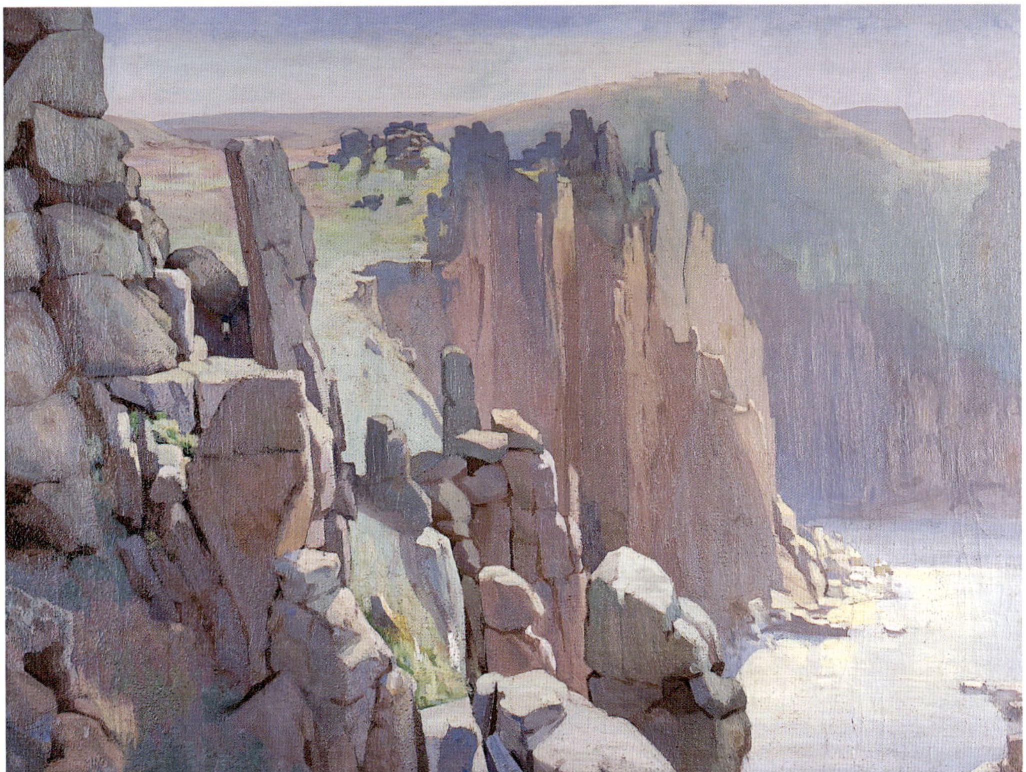
C.NAPER

Ella playing her mouth organ at Dozmary
Charles Naper
Oil on canvas, 16 x 14 in

BELOW
The Hut, Dozmary
Charles Naper
Oil on board, 12 x 16 in

OPPOSITE
Cottages, Sennen
Charles Naper
Oil on board 12 x 14 in

Clifftop Thrift
Charles Naper
Oil on board, 12 x 16 in

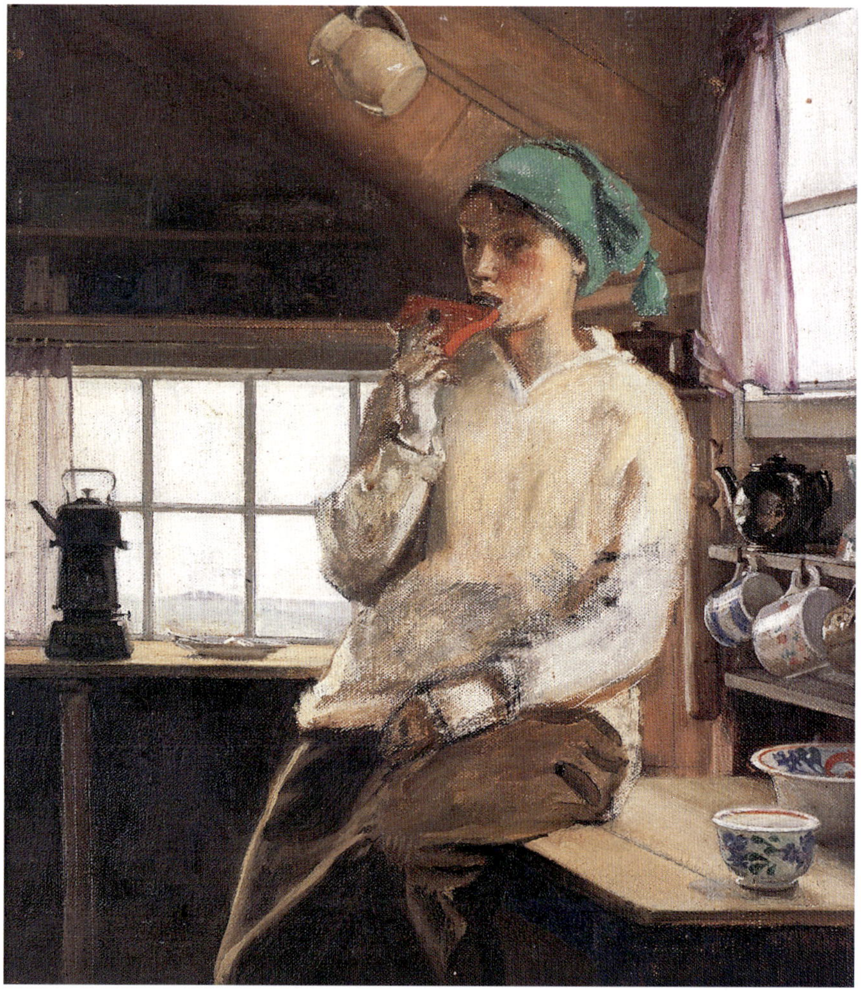

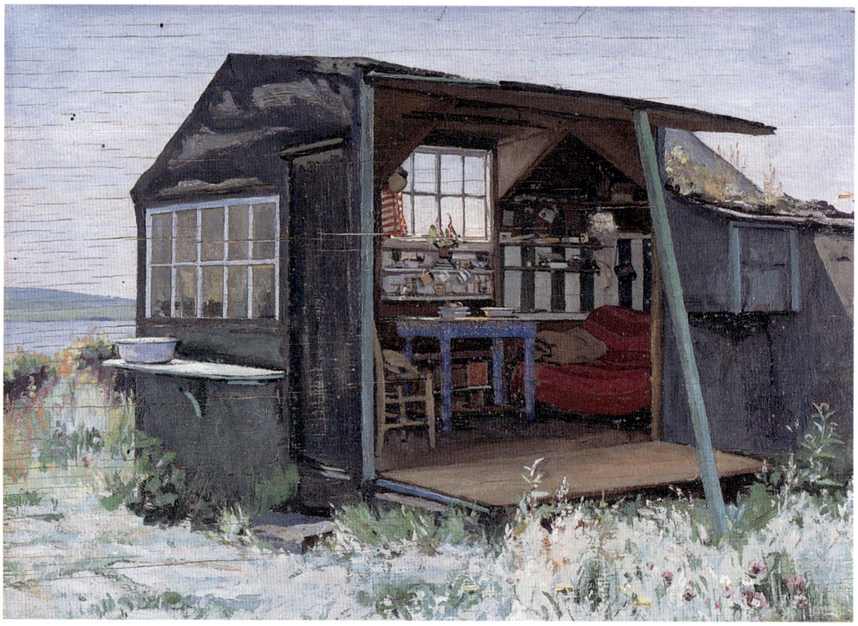

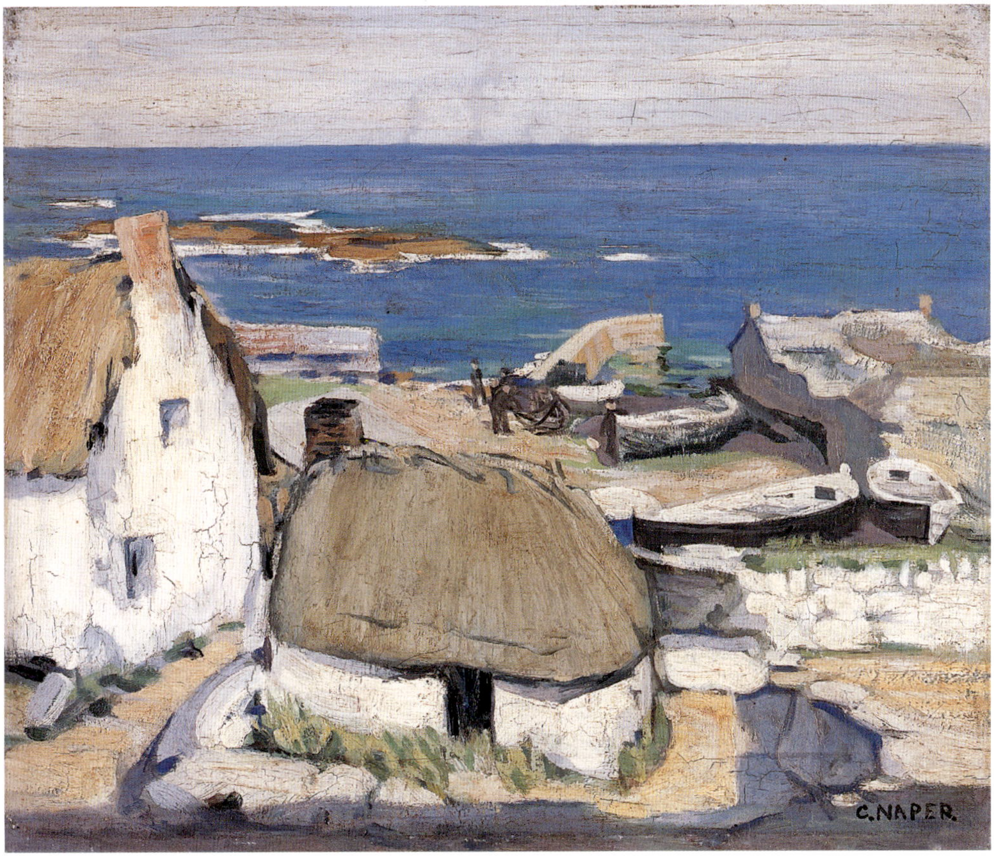
C.NAPER.

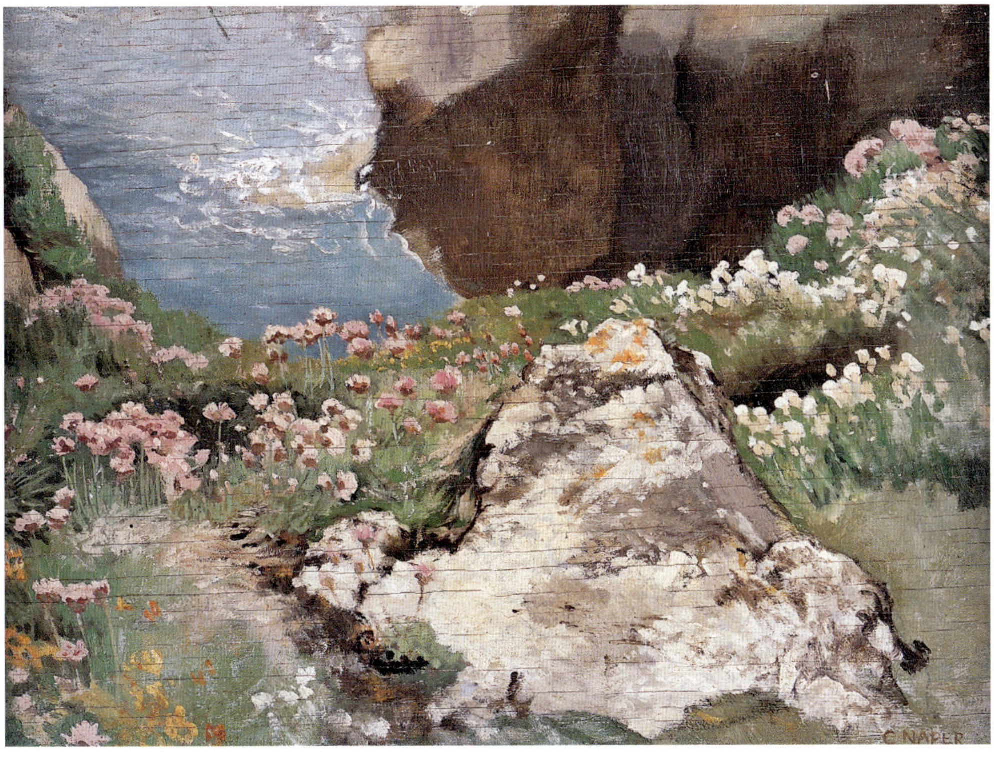
C.NAPER

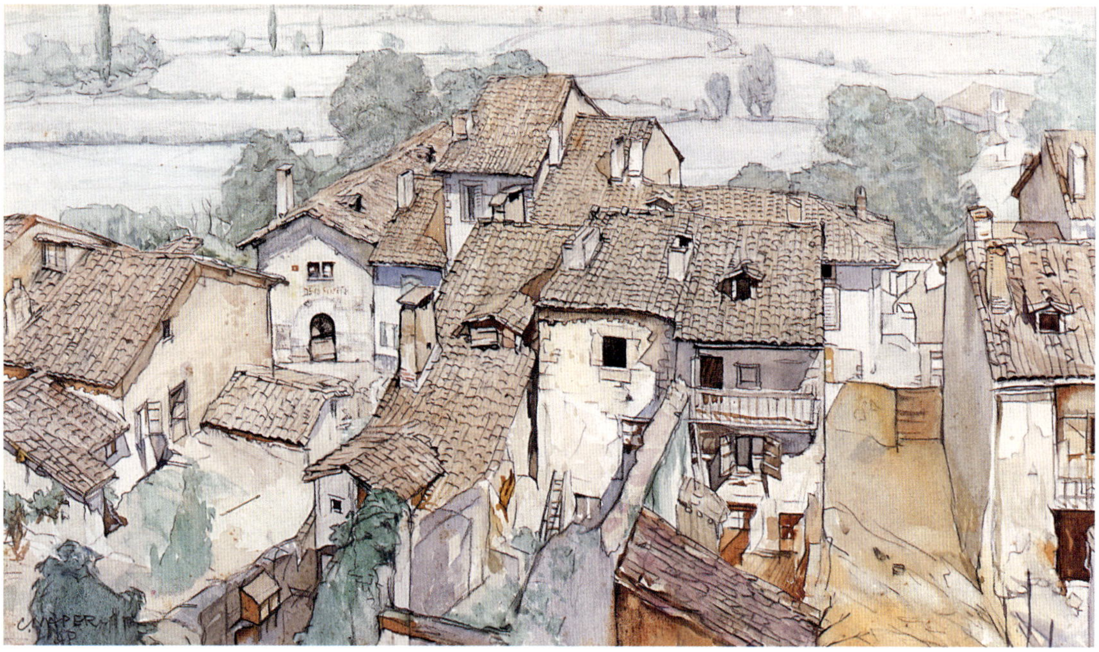

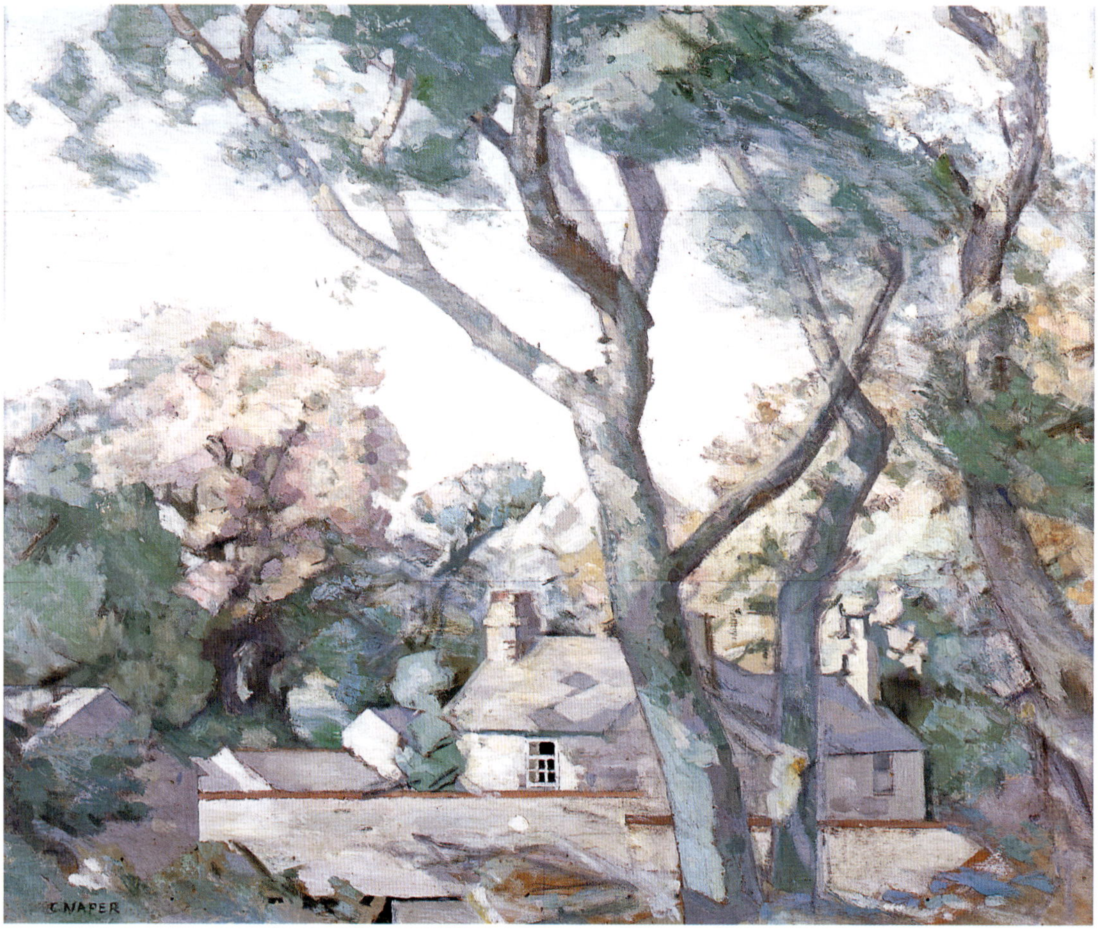
C NAPER

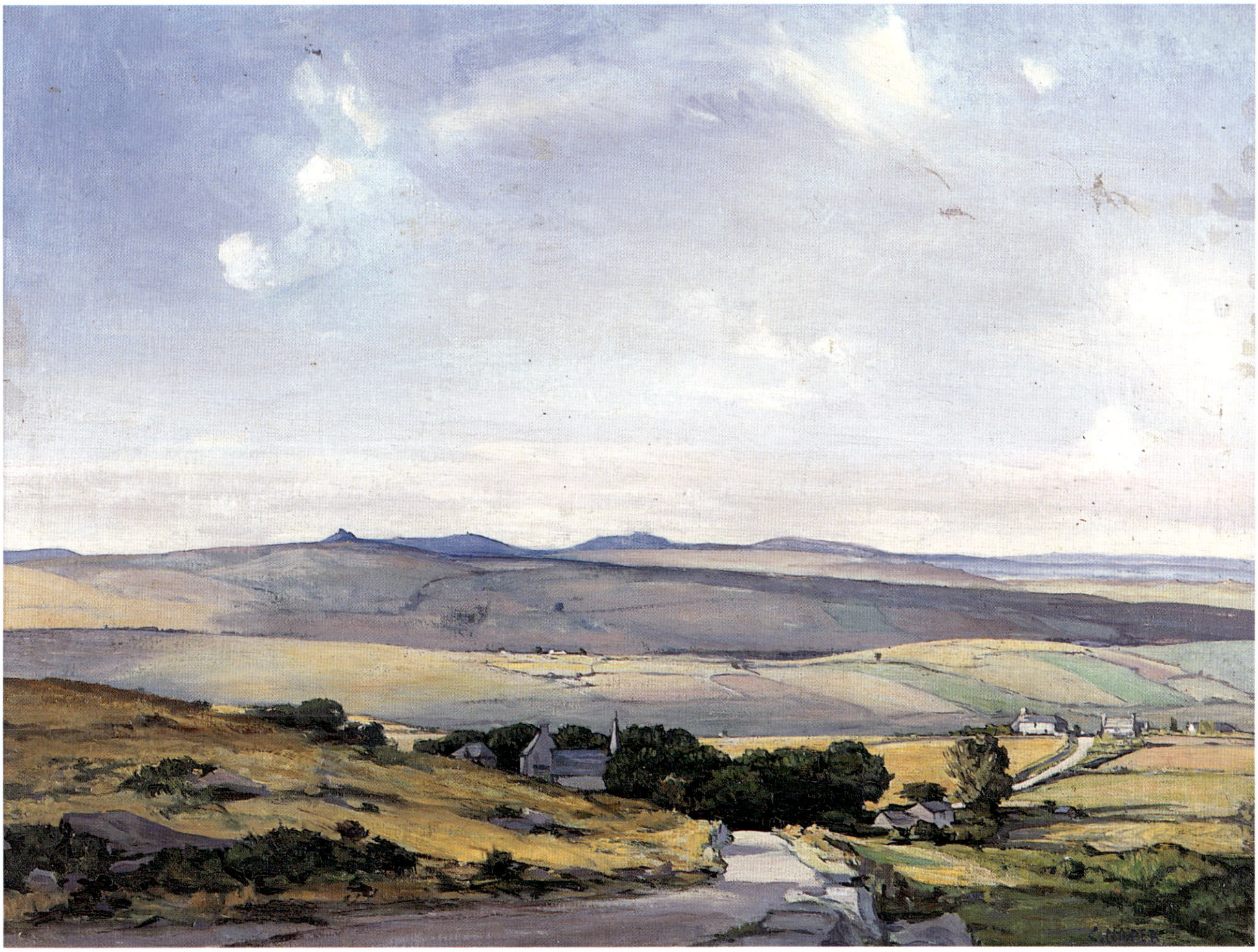

Bodmin Moor
Charles Naper
Oil on canvas, 18 x 24 in

OPPOSITE
Alpine Village
Charles Naper
Watercolour, 9 x 15 in

Trewoofe Farm
Charles Naper
Oil on board, 20 x 24 in

TOP
A flight of butterflies in carved horn and applied shell, possibly for use as a hair ornament

MIDDLE
Silver brooches set with hardstones and semiprecious stones, some enhanced with enamel

BOTTOM
LEFT A silver pendant, green enamelled and set with green chalcedony.
RIGHT A silver pendant set with green abalone shell and four green cabochon stones

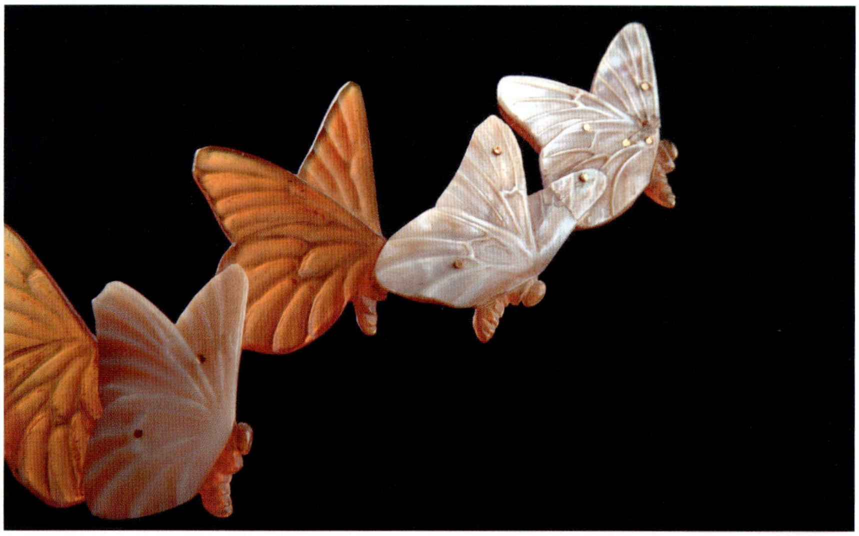

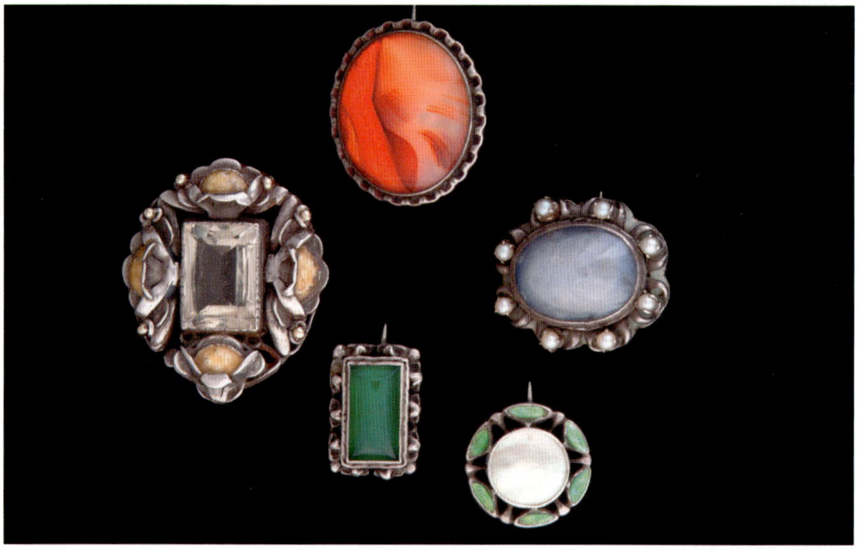

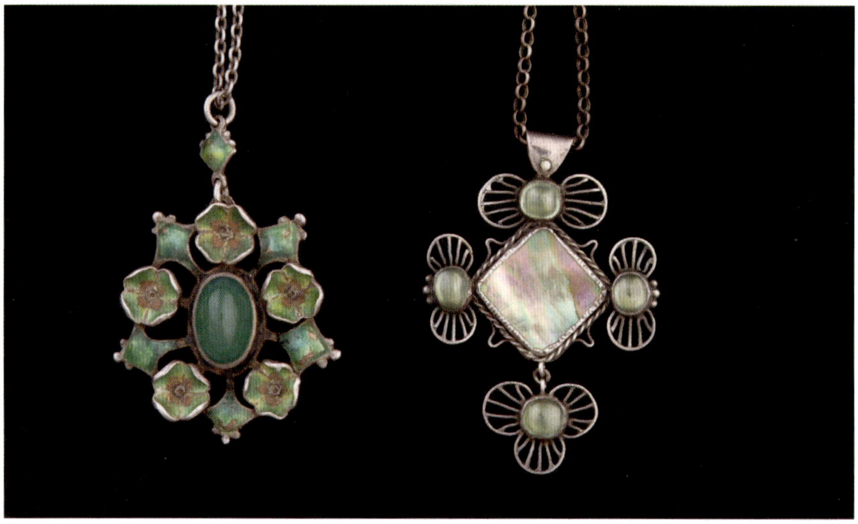

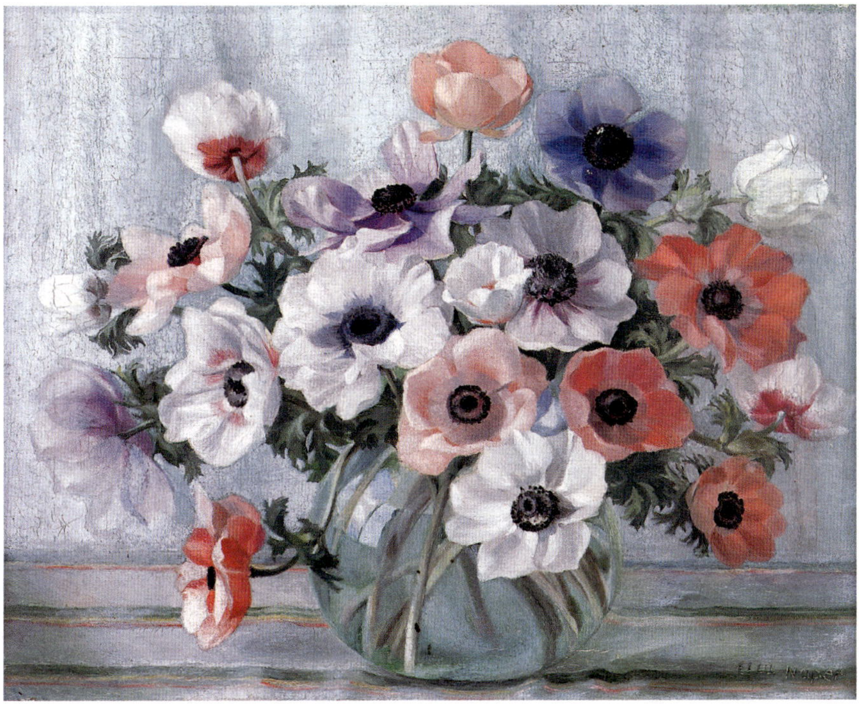

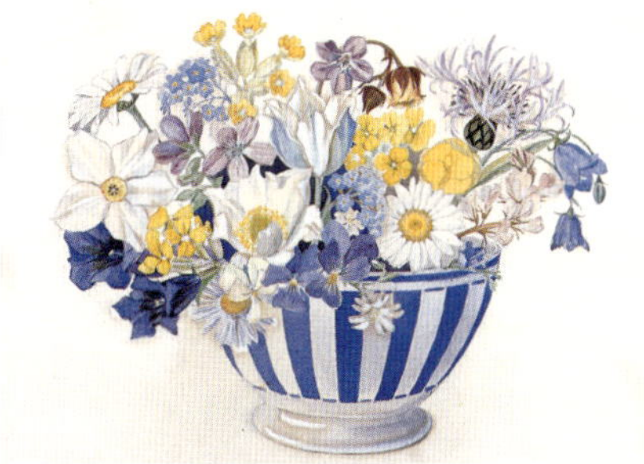

ABOVE
Spring Flowers in Bowl
Ella Naper
Watercolour, $8\frac{1}{2}$ x $10\frac{1}{2}$ in

LEFT
Anemones
Ella Naper
Oil on canvas, $12\frac{1}{2}$ x $15\frac{1}{2}$ in

BOTTOM
Wild Flowers
Ella Naper
Watercolour, 8 x 6 in

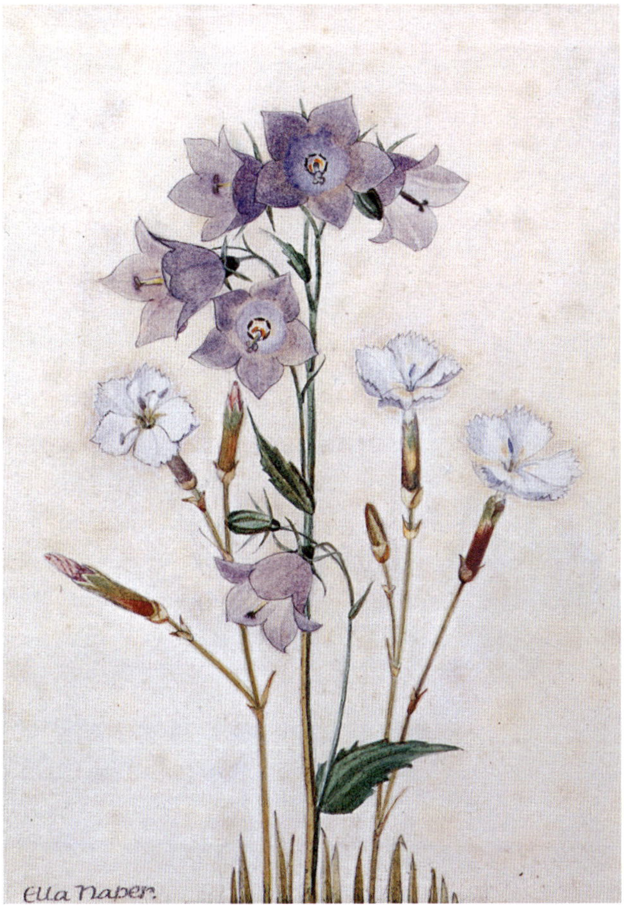

Summer Flowers
Ella Naper
Oil on board

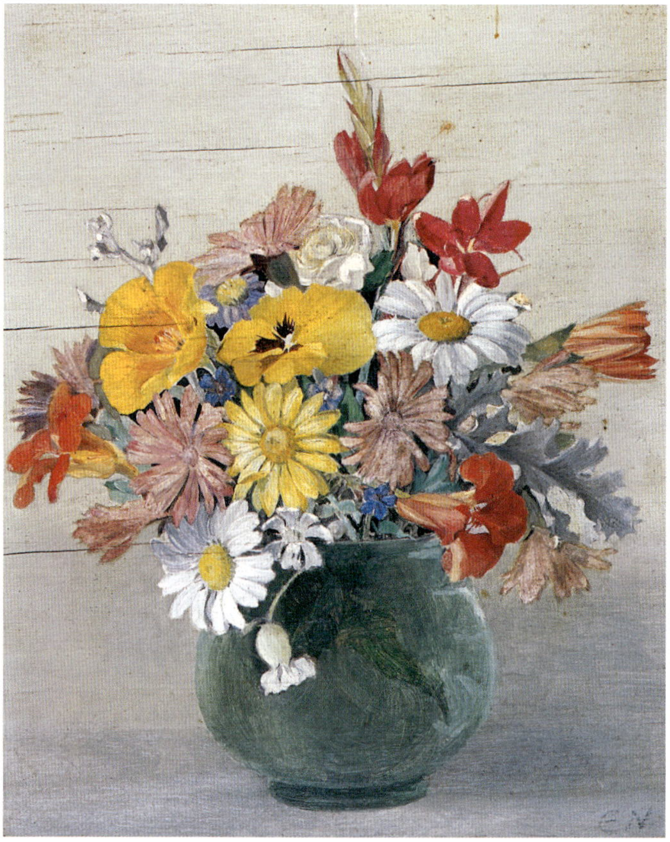

BELOW
Irises and Day Lilies
Ella Naper
Watercolour

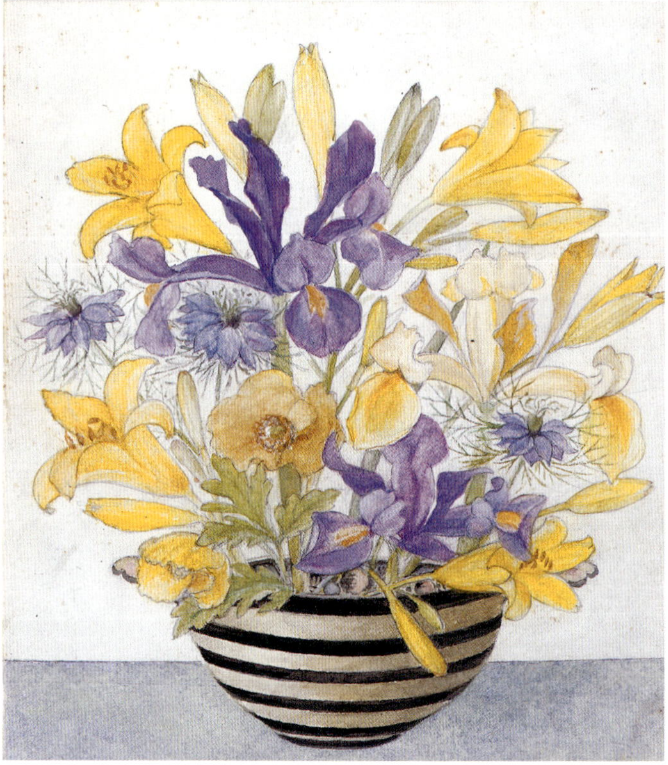

Wild Flowers II
Ella Naper
watercolour

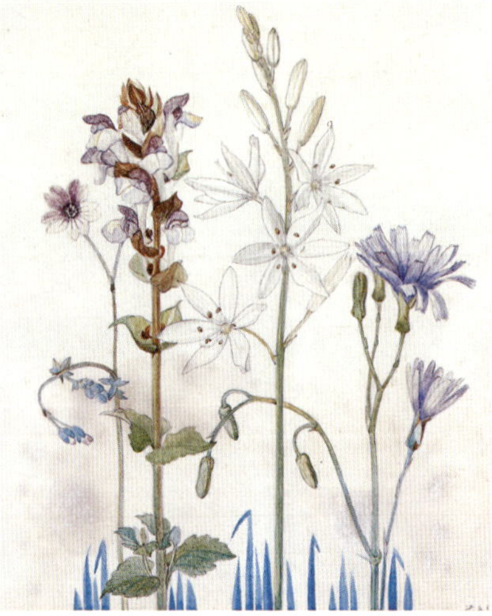

social superiority seemed less important. Ella stayed with her mother-in-law at Ebury Street, London to comfort her. Jane's husband William had died aged eighty-five the previous December and she had to endure the loss of a second son when Frank, a captain in the Lancashire regiment, was killed in France in May 1917. Ella arranged later for Charles Simpson to paint a posthumous portrait of him in his army officer's uniform, done from a photograph. The painting is now in Ireland.

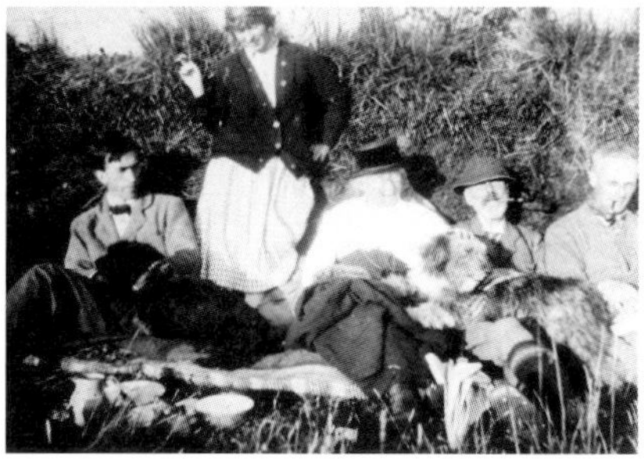

A picnic with Charlie, Laura Knight, the Sidgwicks and Harold Knight

By April 1917 Charlie was still in England and Ella with her family at Lewisham High Road, New Cross. He sent a card from Newmarket to tell 'Dearest darling Ella' that the camp was off altogether. They had packed their kit bags on the cart but the snow was so bad that the show was scratched at the last minute. Ella had been up to Newmarket to see him and he said it was simply lovely having her for the weekend. He was now writing off to Childs (the bankers) for some money. Ella was thinking of going back to Cornwall and he urged her to do just as she wanted.

When she returned to Lamorna Ella was still reluctant to sleep in the house on her own and, as the Knights had done before her, she stayed with her neighbours at Trewoofe Orchard, a short walk away through the farm and down a path beneath trees known as Kale Alley, past the herb gardens of the old manor and into the secluded dell where the Sidgwicks had built their home. Professor Sidgwick – an Oxford don, no less; it is remarkable how the myths of Ella's childhood were realised in her life – and his wife Cecily treated Ella as an adopted daughter and she called them Uncle Alfred and Aunt Cis. Laura Knight called them Mr and Mrs Sidgy.

In November Charlie was on his way with his regiment to Italy. From the station at Menton in the south of France he sent two postcards given him by an English girl on the platform. He writes that it has been a lovely day for seeing everything and that they are progressing very slowly with many stops. 'Let Mother know,' he adds as a postscript. A week later his mother, now clearly reconciled to her daughter-in-law, writes from Exeter on black-edged notepaper, a chatty, friendly letter though she is still in mourning. 'Have you heard from Charlie?' she immediately asks. She is rather anxious as her nephew in the 8th Devons is on his way to Italy and she fears Charlie may be too, though she is relieved that the fighting may not be so bad there as in France.

The elder Mrs Naper was well-informed about the situation on the Italian Front. Italy had made a secret treaty by which it was promised territories on its north-east frontier in return for support of the allies. It declared war on Austria-Hungary and Germany and in October 1917 was heavily defeated in an area fifty miles east of Venice. The Italian government appealed for help and Charlie was in the British force sent to give support. By the time he arrived the offensive had come to an end, the Germans being preoccupied by the western front. Charlie saw little or no fighting, spending the winter strengthening the defences of the new line. He had his photograph taken in St Mark's Square, Venice, surrounded by pigeons, one of which is perched on his hand. The square is deserted, the façade of the cathedral barricaded up. He looks very much the British officer in his pith helmet and uniform, collar and tie, tunic with a Sam Browne belt, riding breeches and puttees.

Before the next Austrian assault in the summer, which involved fierce fighting and heavy casualties, Charlie was on his way home, in March 1918 writing that he is 'going the riviera way again and enjoying every minute of it'. He sent a card of the church at Montivilliers to Trewoofe and it was forwarded to Sennen Cove. Ella's reason for being in Sennen rather than Lamorna might have surprised him.

Harold Knight had never really been in love with Laura. He was a seventeen-year-old student at Nottingham School of Art when the thirteen-year-old Laura was admitted a year earlier than the normal age of entry. Harold was recognised as the most gifted of the class, expected to have a brilliant career. Laura set up her easel behind him, copied his every move and attached herself to him. She always wanted to marry him. Harold more or less got used to having her around; he was quite fond of her, even though he was often irritated by her constant chatter. When in 1903 her painting *Mother and Child* was accepted by the Royal Academy and immediately bought for twenty pounds by one of the academicians, Laura thought it was financial security enough for them to marry. Harold, who had never had any other girlfriend, was persuaded. He had grown up in an extremely repressive family, even by Victorian standards; he seemed cold and remote, focused only on his art. When he finally fell in love with Ella it disturbed him greatly. She was already married to Charlie, he to Laura. Although the artistic community was considered bohemian, their sexual morality was fairly conventional, and his love was a source of anguish to Harold.

He made drawings of Ella, he painted her at Dozmary and in the studio, clothed and unclothed. When Charlie was away and she returned to London he wrote to her: 'Do you want any money, please let me know at once if you do, I am fairly flush as we have sold the car for £108.'

Harold is often represented as a comically puritanical figure, never joining in the dances and parties of pre-war Lamorna. But he was a deeply sincere person and a committed pacifist during the war. He made no secret of his beliefs and this made him very unpopular in a community where many were fighting and dying for their country. Most thought his behaviour selfish and cowardly, that he was a traitor. They refused to recognise him, turned their backs or looked the other way when they met him.

When his call-up papers came he was forty-three and not a well man. If he had been examined he would almost certainly have been turned down as unfit for military service. Laura went to Plymouth to get a doctor's opinion, an act which angered Harold. He refused to go to an army medical. He believed that international disputes should be settled by negotiation, not by fighting, and standing by his principles he chose to appear before a tribunal. He was ordered to work on the land. He went to a farm on the north coast, hoeing the fields in bitter weather, his hands blistered and calloused so badly that he could not paint. He was shunned by the community, alone and miserable. He turned to Ella for desperately needed sympathy. It was a quality which she had in large measure and which she was able to give him. There was nothing she could do for Charlie, away in Italy. She could, though, give Harold the comfort and peace of mind that he could not get from his wife. Laura recognised that she herself offered only anger with Harold for being so high-minded – the whole situation could have been avoided – and absolute rage with their other so-called friends for what she saw as their ignorance and disloyalty. The two people she loved most in the world were Harold and Ella; she could accept the situation.

They needed a bolt-hole away from the gossip of the village, but they could not go far as Harold's movements were restricted by a court order. All Ella's vitality and organising skills went into arranging a solution. The Sidgwicks would do anything for Ella, the daughter they had never had. Lamorna Birch thought that Alfred Sidgwick was looking frail and in need of some 'real old English food' after the years of deprivation. The Sidgwicks let it be known that what they really needed was 'a snug little retreat' where they could get away from Lamorna. It is impossible to know whether they were in collusion with Ella or manipulated by her. They were getting on in years, already had their own snug retreat at Trewoofe Orchard and no need nor energy for all the work of setting up another home. But they found – or most likely Ella found – a cottage at Sennen Cove near Land's End which they announced they intended to share from time to time with the Napers and with Belle Leader and her children.

At Trewoofe Ella set to work brightening up the furniture that they would take to the cottage, painting it her favourite Lamorna blue and pimpernel red. Early one morning she drove over to Sennen, wearing a flame-coloured dress and sitting high up astride the brightly-painted bedheads, chairs and chests-of-drawers. Belle and her children sat on the driver's seat behind the horse. A shake of the reins and they were away on the seven-mile journey to Sennen and its wide and windy sands, with the Atlantic rollers crashing on the shore, its fresh air and openness after the enclosed and stifling valley.

The very next day as they left the cottage for the beach who should they bump into but their new neighbours who had just arrived at the cottage next door – Laura and Harold Knight! They all expressed surprise at this extraordinary coincidence, set up no doubt by the two women. Here in their 'snug little retreat' Harold could draw strength from Ella's presence.

Nothing in Harold's infrequent correspondence later on refers to their closeness, except for a few lines in a letter of November 1925: 'My dear Ella… I can't say how much we enjoyed seeing you all again, the Trewoofians especially. The only blot was that I never seemed to have an opportunity of seeing you alone, and there was so much I wanted to say'. No doubt he felt that she had saved him from a complete breakdown.

On 11 November 1918 the sirens and hooters of vessels in Penzance harbour could be heard at Lamorna, signalling the end of the war. Neighbours rushed from house to house to make sure that everyone knew. There were celebrations in the evening, and fireworks from ships moored in Mount's Bay.

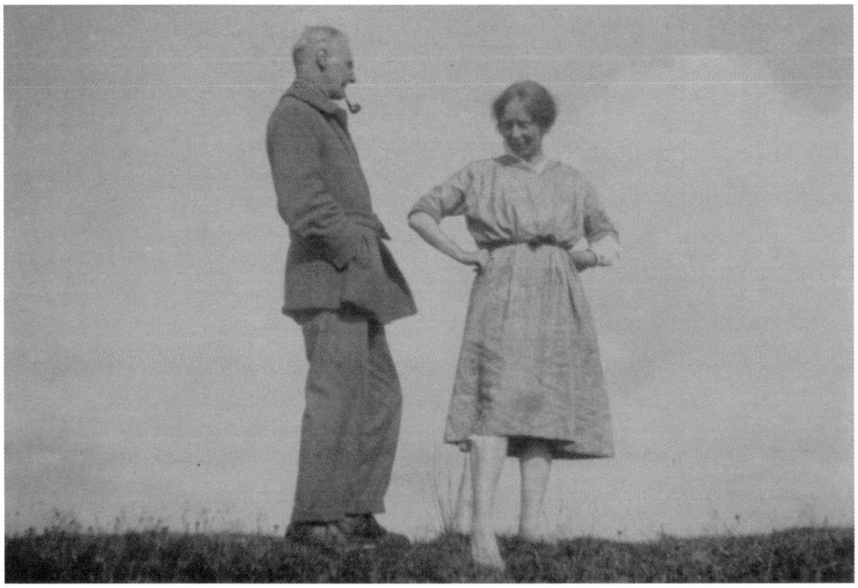

The Art Colony After the War

CHAPTER SIX

Even before the war was over Laura and Harold Knight had decided to move to London. Harold felt that his professional future was in portraiture, at which he was very successful and which could provide them with a good income; it was necessary to be based in London to get commissions. He was also glad to escape the ill-feeling against him in Lamorna and avoid the complications that would follow Charlie's return home. They left in January 1919; Laura was heartbroken to leave Ella and Cornwall.

There was a sense of new beginnings. Ella had her war memorial commissions to work on. She had not done much lettering since carving the motto around the lid of the sewing box that she had made as a student in 1905 and since engraving her 'Ex Libris'. Arts and Crafts lettering was inspired by medieval manuscripts; she needed a more modern style and she bought two recent books on lettering and alphabets. Ella's post-war style is more upright and linear.

Memorial tablets of the period are not usually great works of art, many being produced mechanically by firms of monumental masons and engravers. But Ella's memorial to Benjie Leader is a gem. St Buryan church, its high fifteenth-century tower dominating the Land's End peninsula, is large and bare, with tall granite arcades and an intricately carved rood screen that spans the width of the building. The memorial is situated on the north wall, between and below two windows. It has a wide wooden frame, simple flat boards without moulding and painted black. This encloses the silvery black of a pewter panel about twelve inches high and fifteen inches wide. Three brightly-coloured enamel shields stand out against the tin, the top centre shield being the arms of the regiment, a yellow lamb and flag on a white ground, flanked by two other red, yellow, white and blue coats-of-arms. Around the panel is a band in a design of roses and entwining leaves, with a small shield in the centre of the base containing Leader's initials BEL.

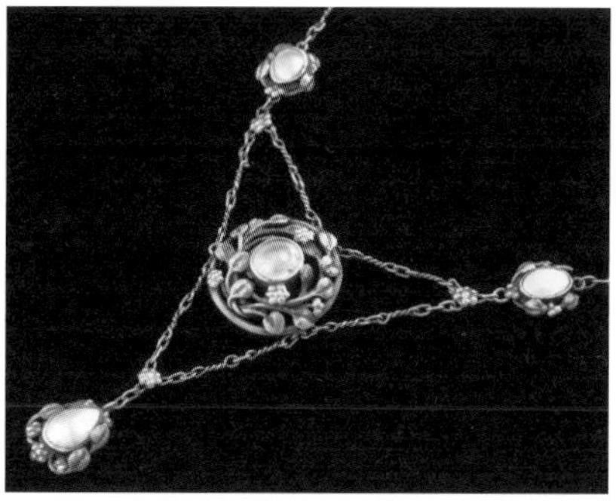

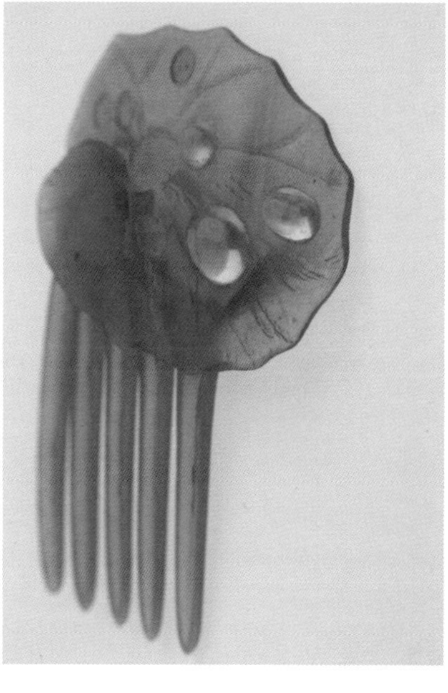

TOP
The necklace Ella made for Ruth Simpson

Lily pad comb (see page 86)

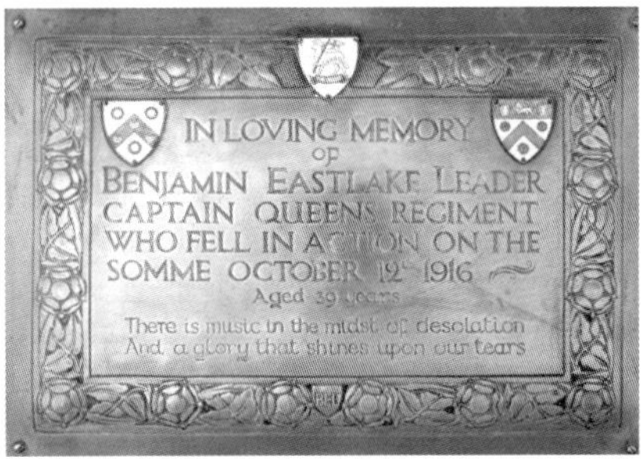

Ella's memorial tablet to Benjamin Leader

IN LOVING MEMORY

OF

BENJAMIN EASTLAKE LEADER

CAPTAIN QUEENS REGIMENT

WHO FELL IN ACTION ON THE

SOMME OCTOBER 12TH 1916

Aged 39 years

There is music in the midst of desolation

And a glory that shines upon our tears

The work is signed in very small letters in the bottom right-hand corner ELLA NAPER. It is a very individual piece, full of delicacy and feeling.

Much less personal is the tablet by the West Door of Exeter Cathedral, in memory of nine Devonshire men from a gun battery of the Royal Field Artillery. It is entirely in lettering, with a bronze sheen on the embossed letters against a dark background. A more elaborate design was executed for the James family of Plymouth. Edward James had been mayor of Plymouth and two of his grandsons died at Loos in Flanders in 1915. It was placed in Charles church, Plymouth, and was destroyed in the bombing raids on the city in the Second World War. Her full-scale plans survive, done in pencil on the back of one of Charlie's architectural studies for the sake of economy, some seventy words, each letter of which is meticulously drawn, the shields and badges coloured.

As part of their fresh start Ella tried to be more methodical in keeping accounts, though they tailed off after a few years. She wrote FISH on the cover of a little red notebook; it contains a month by month record of the fish they caught, with the date and weight. It begins seriously enough – 1 bass, 1 flatfish, 1 small turbot, 'line got tangled with 2 others, took hours to undo' – but jokes begin to appear. Amongst the fish caught in August 1919 are 2 lager and 3 ginger beer. In October 'lancing commences. Charlie in good spirits.' They caught 3 pollack, 1 catfish (which they put back) and 1 cold. On 20 October they put the spiller out with Uncle Alfred and Crosbie Garstin and caught 14 cwt of seaweed, 1 old boot and a dead cat. 'Not a very good month for lances.' The fishing is over by November and Charlie plans to take up apple culture. Ella notes that 'if it had not been for the frequent gifts of fish from kind Mr Nicholls to me I don't know what we should have done'.

She began, more seriously, to make up her business ledger, having abandoned it at the beginning of the war, the last entries being seven items

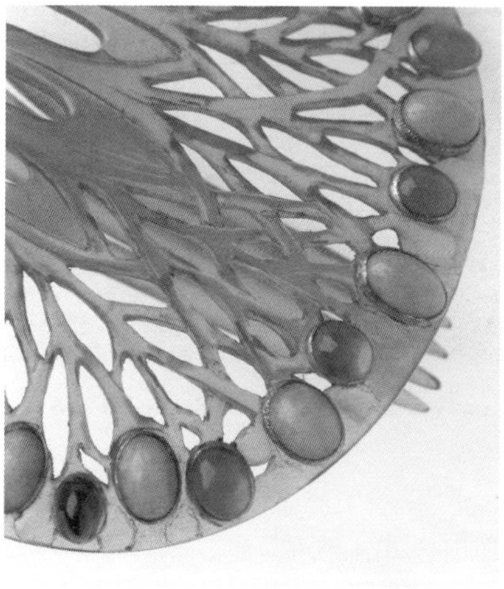

A carved and pierced horn hair comb, the border set with green hardstones and chalcedony, made for 'Mouse'

sent to the Brighton Guild of Applied Art in 1914. In the first months of 1920 she sold a ring for five guineas, a pendant for seven and a chain to Mrs Sergeant for four. Grosvenor Galleries paid her twelve guineas, a Mr Burney bought four pendants for £38.19.0, Ruth Simpson paid £2.10.0 for her pendant – the price to a friend – and Mrs Bolitho at Trengwainton bought a silver box set with gold and jade for seven guineas. The summer must have been devoted to fishing and gardening, as well as preparing work for the winter exhibitions. In November she exhibited at the 'Englishwoman's' and sold some twenty-six pieces, hairpins set with moons and enamel, greenhorn buckles, rings and pendants set with cornelian and pearls, amethyst and moonstones, rose quartz and blue chalcedony, a bracelet set with plique à jour enamel, brooches and cuff-links.

They were priced at two, three or five guineas, a few at eight; the plique à jour enamel, the most difficult of enamelling techniques, was the dearest at ten. In December she sent pins, buckles and combs to Arts and Crafts in Bournemouth and thirty pounds' worth of jewellery to Handicrafts in Beauchamp Place, London. On Christmas Eve, leaving their purchases to the last moment, Capt E. (Gilbert Evans, now back in Lamorna) bought a pair of yellow and gold pins for three guineas, C.G. (Crosbie Garstin) bought a silver and green ring for two guineas and Miss Paynter (Betty, the daughter of Colonel Paynter of Boskenna) had an opal set in a ring for which Ella charged three guineas. Her total income from jewellery for the year amounted to £192.15.0. When the cost of her materials is taken into account, this is no more than a village schoolteacher's salary, just enough for them to live on with gifts of fish from kind Mr Nicholls.

The necklace that Ella made for Ruth in 1920 has a medallion with a mother of pearl centre hanging on a silver chain surrounded by three balanced and suspended small circlets, like moons around a planet. For Lamorna Birch's wife Houghton, known as 'Mouse', she made a comb of amber-tinted horn, the intricate branches ending in a canopy of blue and turquoise stones.

There is no record of Charlie earning anything in 1920 and even his fishing was not very successful. He may have sent off to Childs for money from time to time, but the funds on which he could draw were limited. Ella was the breadwinner, a very unusual situation in those days.

Social life resumed in Lamorna though it was less exuberant than before the war. When Alfred Munnings and Laura Knight were there, the parties had been boisterous. Munnings took complete control of the entertainment, singing hunting songs and making everyone else join in the choruses which

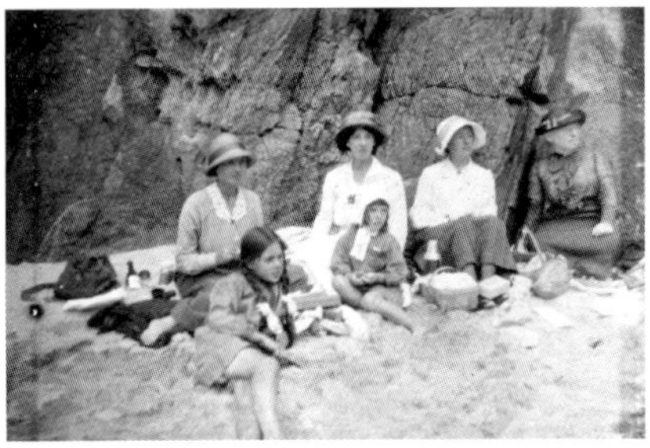

Ella and the Birches at Nanjizal

he taught them. He recited poems with enormous gusto, Edgar Allan Poe's *The Raven* being his speciality. Another party piece was *The Tale of Anthony Bell*, a hunting ballad in sixty verses that he composed mainly on horseback in the Lamorna valley. Everyone – except Harold Knight – was captivated by his vitality. Parties were held at Mrs Jory's Cliff House Hotel, but after the suicide of his wife Florence there in 1914 Munnings returned less often.

However, there was still plenty of social contact and movement to and fro between the artists' homes and studios. Musical evenings were held at Flagstaff Cottage and Bodriggy, the home of the landscape painter Algernon Newton whose wife played the piano. There is a photograph of a luncheon party in Charles Simpson's studio at St Ives, taken soon after the end of the war. Simpson stands, a cigarette between his lips and drawing a cork from a bottle, while a dozen guests sit around two tables. Ruth Simpson sits in front of him, next to Eleanor Hughes, both wearing wide-brimmed hats of a pre-war style. 'Ella Naper is on the right.' There are two young women dressed more fashionably than the others on the right. One sits in a low armchair, very erect in the uncomfortable seat, her hands clasped over her knee. She hides the woman behind her, whose cloche hat is covered with a material of a bold floral pattern, tied at the back; the same material is at her neck, beneath a dark jacket. She holds a tumbler of wine to her lips, a cigarette in her left hand. This is all more characteristic of Ella; the other figure seems prim and tense and is perhaps a student of the Simpsons at the Shoreline Studio, where Charles taught landscape painting and Ruth portraiture. Professor and Mrs Sidgwick, Alfred white-bearded and Cecily heavy-bosomed, sit on the left; they would have brought Ella over to St Ives.

Ruth Simpson painted her portrait of Ella at this time. Laura Knight had portrayed her as a naked body, Harold Knight in *Dozmare Pool* 1916 as a symbol. Charles had painted her in her twenties in the hut on Bodmin Moor: fey, gypsy-like, romantic. Ruth captures the personality of Ella in her thirties. She sees a woman who is very self-assured, even bold; she seems almost to flaunt herself. Ella is shown in half-figure against a deep red background. She wears a close-fitting dress with a deep V at the neck in a bold abstract design of red chevrons on a deep blue ground. She adopts her typical stance when posing, her elbow at an angle, her left hand resting palm outwards on her hip. She looks cheeky, humorous, full of vitality; a mature and self-confident woman.

Visitors to the Hughes' were likely to play euchre, the card game so popular in Cornwall and the subject of a painting by Henry Scott Tuke. At the Sidgwicks they played chess. Alfred Sidgwick competed with Tom Gotch in Newlyn by correspondence, sending the moves on a postcard. He also played against Charlie, often in the garden of Trewoofe Orchard where Mrs Sidgy had her writing hut. The game at the Napers' was ping-pong; there was a table in the studio and scores were kept on the cupboard doors. Later they played bridge, and scrabble when they were on their own. Ella made a drawstring bag for the letters, embroidered with red and blue flowers. The company at Trewoofe Orchard was more intellectual, with philosophers and writers often coming down to spend the weekend.

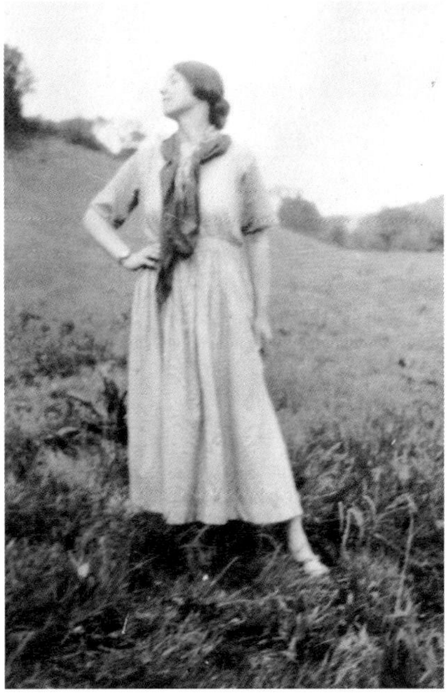

Ella in a characteristic pose

When the Knights returned for the summer to camp out in the studio, they brought with them W.H. Davies. He was a celebrity since the publication of *The Autobiography of a Super Tramp*; they had met whilst dining at the Café Royal in London. He lazed about all day but came into his own in the evenings when he put the skills he had learned on the road into organising a bonfire. He had everyone collecting wood and the blaze attracted the whole of Lamorna, Ella amongst them. The poetry she liked was romantic and mystical, celebrating the awe and majesty of Nature. Davies's poems were simple, almost naïve, and the author of 'What is this life if, full of care, we have no time to stand and stare' turned out to be remarkably ignorant of the countryside. He called all birds robins and did not know the difference between hay and straw. He was a bit of a disappointment and was never seen writing anything in the whole summer he spent at Lamorna. When his *Farewell to Poesy* came out in a second edition in 1921, he inscribed a copy 'To Ella Naper'.

Hubert and Nancy Wellington also came down in the summer, staying at Sennen. There are photographs of them in front of the same striped beach tent that they had at Looe, Hubert's hair long and bushy and parted in the middle, Nancy's short and curly. He made a pen-and-ink sketch of Ella and Nancy asleep on the sand at Nanjizal, with Ella's Pekinese Minchi Fu curled up between them. Wellington was a member of the Camden Town Group of painters and the Napers had two of his pictures, one of an empty meadow and another of a flat-topped wagon standing in a field. He wrote on art for the *Spectator* and *Manchester Guardian* and was Registrar of the Royal College of Art until he was appointed Principal of the Edinburgh College of Art in 1932. He was very progressive and outward looking, introducing his students to modern ideas. He used grants from benefactors to enable students to travel and study abroad, and it was through his influence that Wilhelmina Barns-Graham, one of his post-graduate students, came to St Ives in 1940. Hubert Wellington is a link between an older generation of

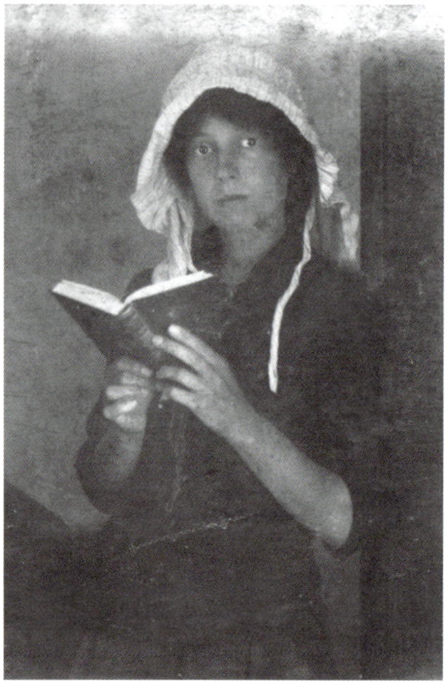

TOP
Ella posing

Spring 1916
Laura Knight
Oil on canvas, 60 x 72 in

artists and a younger, between the traditionalists and the moderns. He was in touch with both worlds, but kept them quite separate. After Nancy's death Hubert married Irene, one of his students, and Irene and Ella became good friends.

One summer Charlie and Ella went to the French Alps on a painting holiday. Charlie sketched the high mountains and deep valleys around Gap, the ancient rocks that he always loved. Whether in Cornwall or the Alps, he also favoured views looking down on the rooftops of villages. Ella posed for the camera in Alpine pastures. Her photograph album at Trewoofe was home-made like so many things in the house. It consisted of sheets of brown paper, the sort for wrapping parcels, held between the hard covers of an old sketching-pad. There are photos of the building of the house, the clearing of the garden and leat, holidays at Dozmary with the Knights and the Harveys, picnics with the Birches and the Hughes, outings in Cornwall with the Wellingtons and the Sidgwicks. Ella always assumed a pose if she saw the camera turned on her. It is invariably graceful, as though it came naturally to her. Very occasionally it seems more 'artistic'. Her characteristic pose is preserved in the photographs, in Ruth Simpson's portrait and in Laura Knight's painting *Spring*.

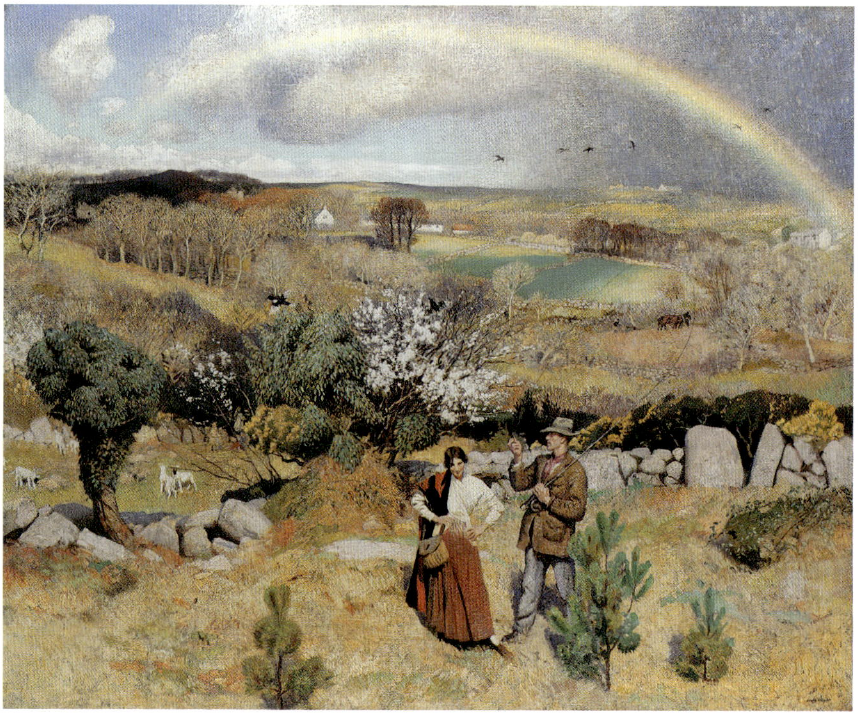

Ella and Gluck

CHAPTER SEVEN

The artist Gluck had a studio not far from the Napers, just below the turning down into the valley amongst the trees near the stream. In the twenties she painted at least three pictures with Ella as the subject. Hannah Gluckstein had first visited Lamorna as a twenty-year-old student from St John's Wood Art School, staying in 1915 at Rosemerrin, up the lane from the Hugheses and the home of Benjie and Belle Leader. She had been born into the family that founded the J. Lyons and Co catering empire, a wealthy Jewish background against which she rebelled. She rejected the family name, insisting on being known by the single syllable 'Gluck'. She liked to wear clothes that outraged her conventional family. She relished the bohemian atmosphere of Lamorna, and was accepted into it. 'It was an incredible stroke of luck,' she wrote, 'my first meeting with genuine artists.' Working in the valley were the Knights and the Napers, Birch and Munnings, all of whom she met. She fell for Ella.

Munnings did a drawing of her as a gypsy girl with a clay pipe in her mouth, long flowing hair and skirt, an unusual image as later her hair was always cropped short and she wore men's clothes. 'I was very spoiled by them all because they liked my singing, and we used to have a lot of music in the Knights' huge studio. Little did I think that one day it would be mine.' In the middle of the war she ran away from home to return to Lamorna with a fellow student Craig, who was also known only by her surname.
They rented a cottage and Gluck had a studio. She stayed with Ella and Charles in their hut at Dozmary, where the Knights had added their own hut after the experience of camping in a gale.

Gluck composed the pictures of herself and Ella in the studio from sketches and photographs. She puts herself into the painting, but not as Laura Knight had done in *Self and Nude*, where the artist has paintbrush in hand and is working at her canvas; Gluck includes herself as a character

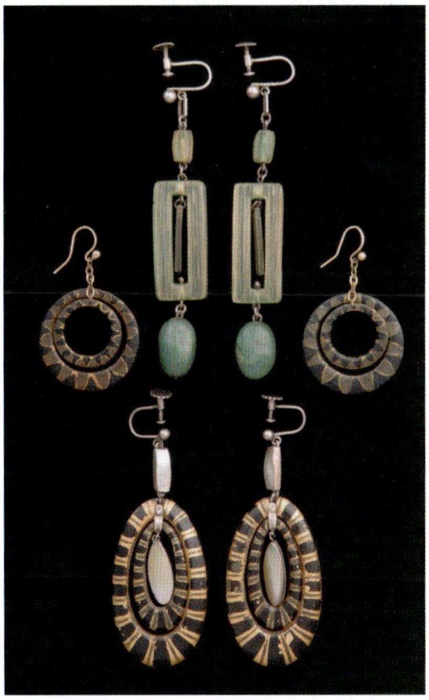

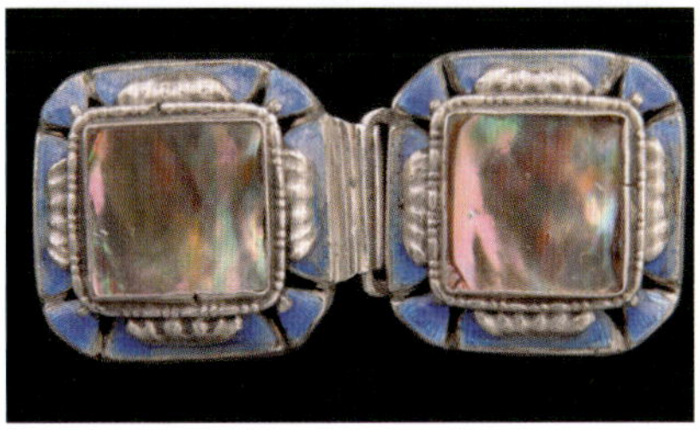

TOP
Pendant earrings in hand-painted horn, incorporating mother of pearl and green-stained horn with jadette

A blue enamelled two-part silver buckle set with ablone shell

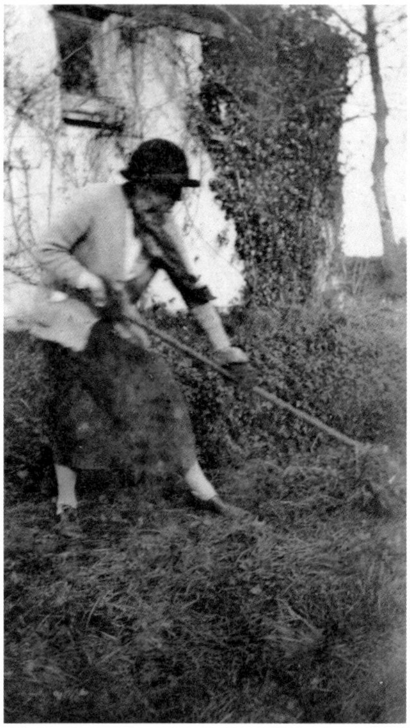

TOP
Photograph of Ella for ***Bonfire***

RIGHT
Bonfire
Gluck (Hannah Gluckstein)
Painting of Gluck watching Ella at work

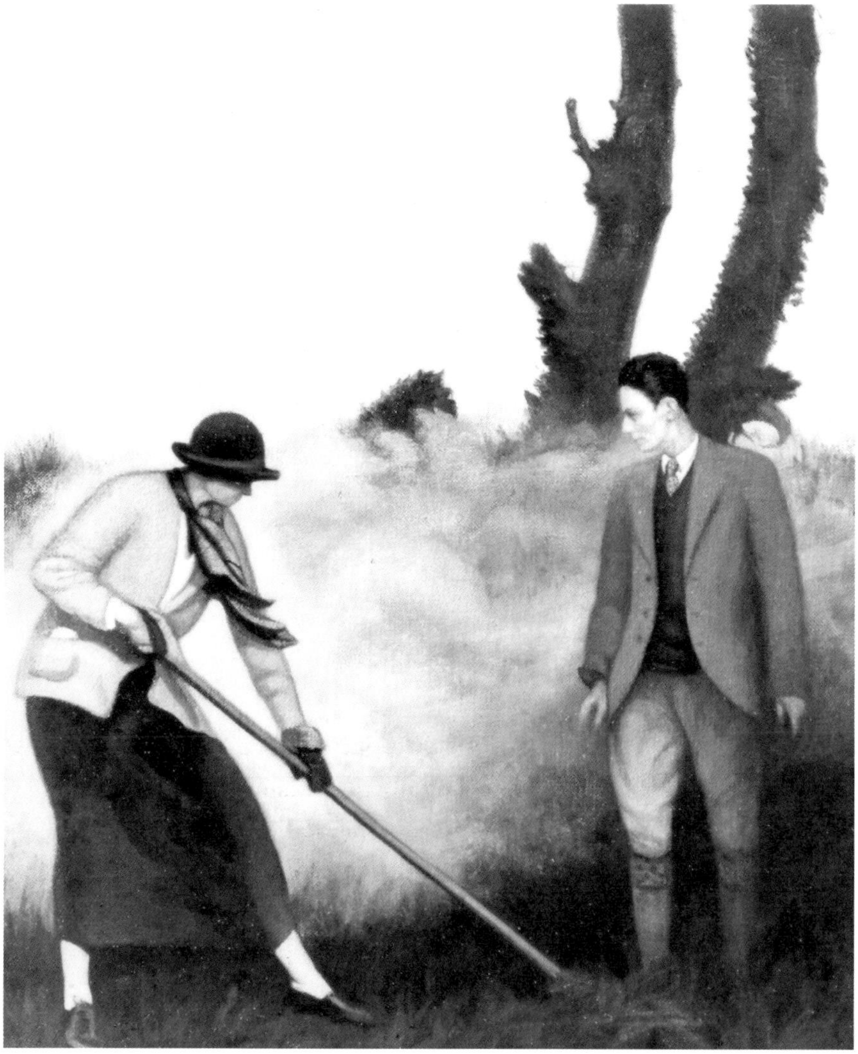

within the scene. In *Bonfire* Ella is raking leaves in her garden, gathering them for burning. She leans forward over the rake, her face half-hidden in shadow beneath a cloche hat. She wears a long cardigan and her skirt, almost to her ankles, is stretched wide between her legs planted well apart. Her silk scarf lifts in the breeze, which swirls the smoke of the bonfire behind her. She looks down, concentrating on the job in hand. On the right of the painting stands Gluck, her dark hair cut short and wearing sports coat and breeches, collar and tie. She looks like a young lord of the manor as she gazes intently at Ella, her hands held stiffly at her sides as though she has to restrain herself from leaping forward and embracing this beautiful, engrossed young woman who pays her no attention at all. The trunks of two trees, jagged with ivy and harshly lopped, rise from her shoulders. They look like enormous horns or antlers and give the picture a very unsettled and awkward feeling, but it conveys strongly the physical passion that Gluck feels for Ella.

Gluck included herself in the drawing of Ella at Dozmary Pool on which was based the painting exhibited in her 'Stage and Country' exhibition at the Fine Art Society in Bond Street in 1926. Ella kneels amongst the sedges to wash clothes in the lake, while Gluck stands just behind her, not domineering or masterful but facing the other direction. When later Gluck fell in love with Nesta Obermer she painted a double portrait of Nesta and herself cheek by jowl, one profile superimposed on the other like a relief sculpture, the two heads merging into one with Nesta's fair hair encircling Gluck's dark Eton crop. The body language in her paintings of Ella makes clear that Gluck's feelings were not reciprocated. A third painting shows Ella standing in a meadow 'in a clinging dress' with her beloved dog Minchi Fu. One suspects that Ella's attention is focused on the dog rather than the artist.

Ella was unperturbed by Gluck. She accepted people as they were, and always enjoyed admiration and being looked at. She had another small photograph album containing nothing but photographs of herself and Gluck taken by each other. In one of them she is raking leaves in the garden, and the pose was transferred quite literally to the canvas for *Bonfire*. This painting has a strange history, itself being condemned to the flames. When Gluck started her love affair with Nesta in 1936 she wanted to destroy all reminders of her past loves. A visitor to her studio at Bolton House in Hampstead said it was like Golders Green crematorium, and the image of Ella was burned. Gluck cut out and kept the fragment of herself.

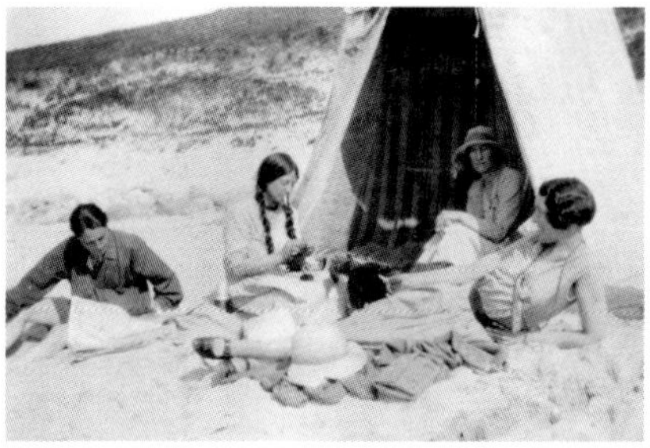

'Sand pit', Sennen: Gluck, Ella and Ruth and Leonora Simpson

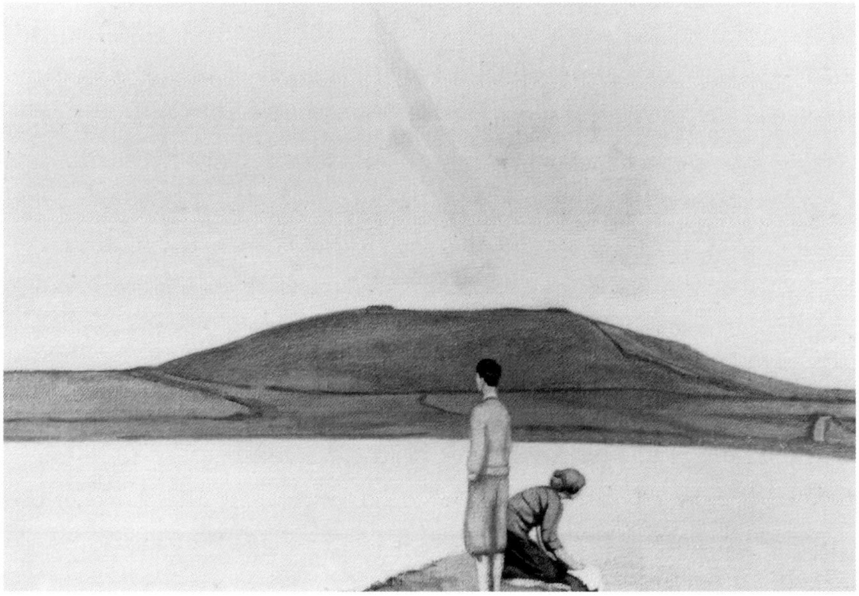

Dozmary
Gluck (Hannah Gluckstein)
© The Artist's Estate

The Dark Pool
Laura Knight
© Reproduced with permission of Curtis Brown Group Ltd, London on behalf of the Estate of Dame Laura Knight.
Copyright © Dame Laura Knight.
Image courtesy of Tyne and Wear Museums Service

The Bathing Pool
Harold Knight
© Reproduced with permission of Curtis Brown Group Ltd, London on behalf of the Estate of Harold Knight.
Copyright © Harold Knight.
Image courtesy of Tyne and Wear Museums Service

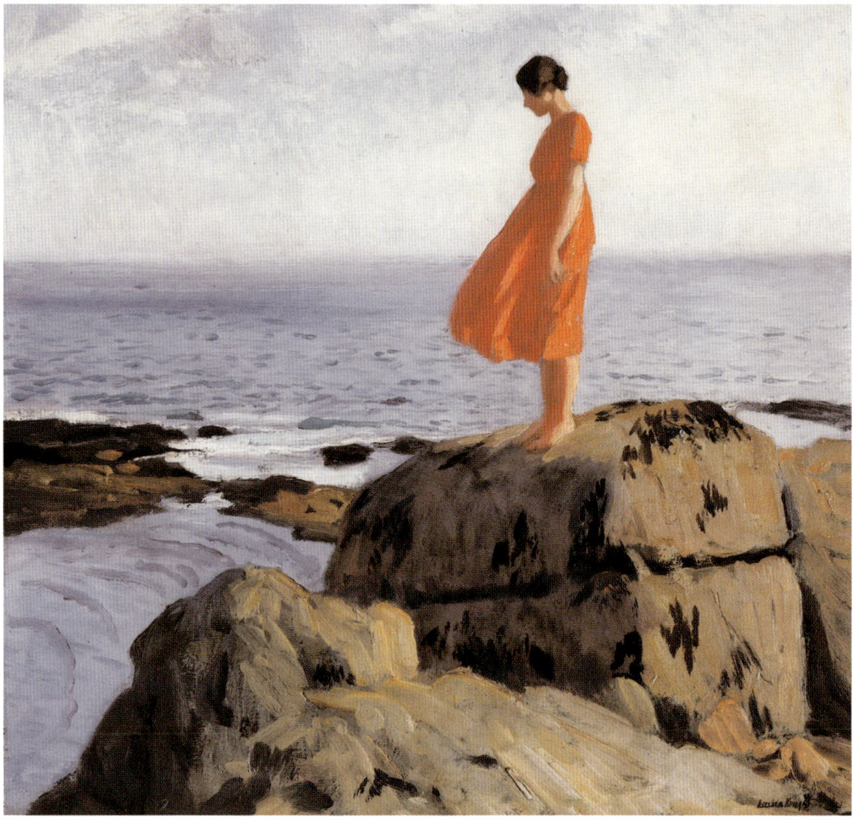

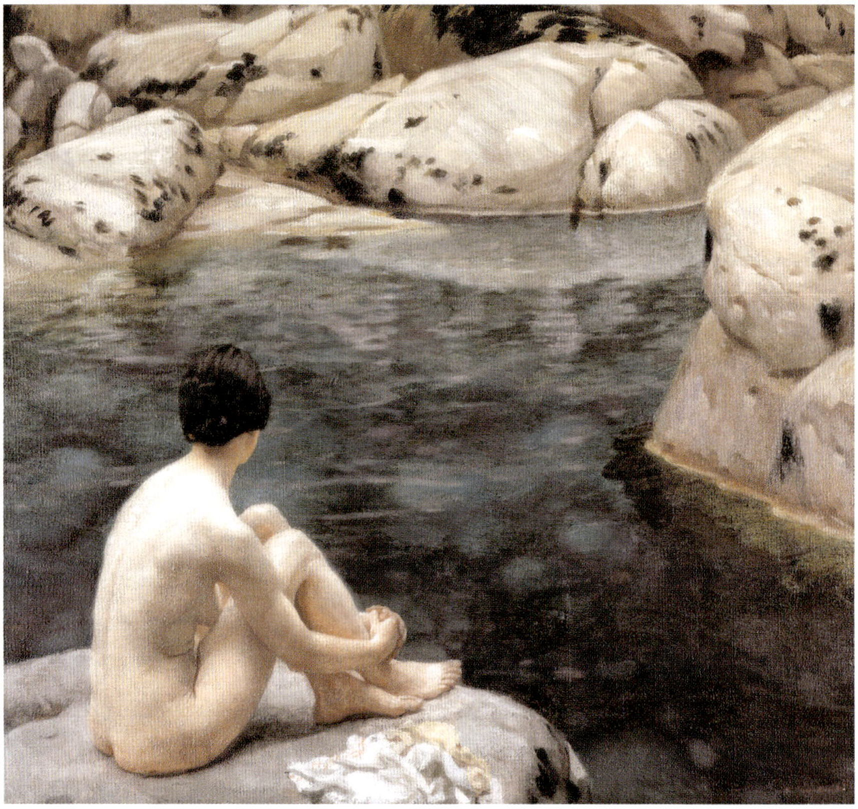

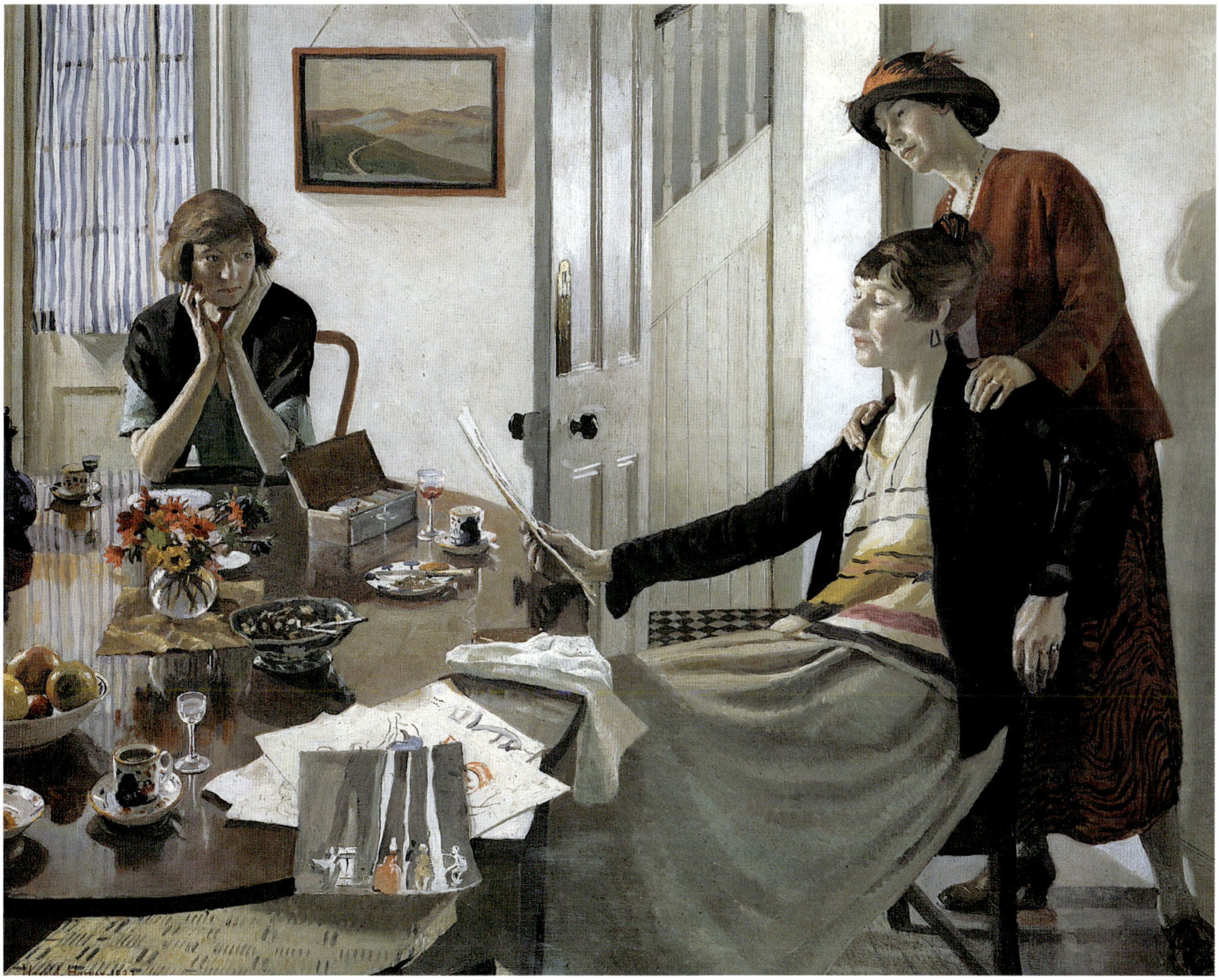

The Critics, 1922
Harold Harvey
Oil on canvas, 23¼ x 29¼ in

Ella could not have known that her portrait had been destroyed, though Gluck always kept a studio at Lamorna, taking over Laura Knight's studio in the late twenties and later owning Dolphin Cottage. She returned for holidays when the two women would meet again, but Gluck is not likely to have told Ella what she had done to the painting. However, whether she knew or not, Ella had a kind of revenge. A quarter of a century after they had both died, a painting of a white farm horse by Kate Westrup which had belonged to Ella was taken out of its frame for cleaning. On the reverse of the backing board, out of sight, was a Gluck painting of black rocks and green sea at Lamorna Cove.

Ella was not an obvious model for her friend Dod Procter, whose paintings of lightly draped statuesque figures were such a success at the Royal Academy in the twenties. But she did pose for Harold Harvey in the interior scenes that he was then painting. In *The Critics* of 1922 two women are studying the paintings of a third, who sits anxiously awaiting their comments. The room is modern and uncluttered, in Harvey's own house, Maen Cottage in Newlyn; the walls are bare, distempered rather than papered, with a single painting in a narrow wooden frame. The circular table is highly polished; on the gleaming surface are a bowl of anemones, bowls of fruit and nuts, a box of cigarettes, coffee cups and empty port glasses. The woman holding the sketch is his wife Gertrude; she looks at it rather superciliously, holding it at arm's length in order to evaluate it. Behind her, with both hands on her shoulders and leaning slightly forwards is Ella Naper. Gertrude looks as though she could be waspish, and the apprehension on the unknown artist's face is probably justified. Ella looks kindly disposed towards the work.

In real life she was a good listener and people confided in her throughout her life. Some thirty years later 'Jan' from Newlyn wrote to say 'what a comforting person you are. I can't tell you how very much better I feel for having had the opportunity of unburdening myself to you yesterday. It was so kind of you to bear with me as I needed to talk to someone and you seem to understand so well all I feel. Thank you, my dear.'

Bob Wellington recalled her warm, vital voice and presence, and the sound of her forthright chuckle and laughter; Pat Male, her warm personality and the air of calm and peacefulness that surrounded her. When Harold Harvey depicted her as the sympathetic one in *The Critics* it was entirely in character.

The Lamorna Pottery

CHAPTER EIGHT

Harold Harvey's paintings show the changing taste in interior design, away from dark furniture and towards simplicity. Charles designed and made some very plain dressing tables, washstands and side tables, with sconces for candlesticks at the side and painted cream. He built a dresser in the kitchen and Ella made ceramic handles.

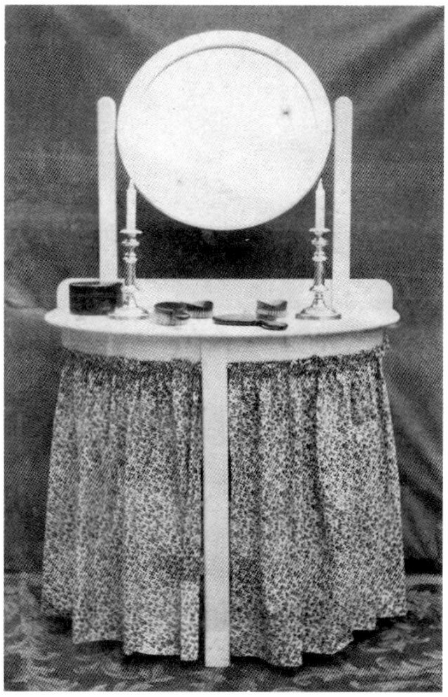

Charlie's home-made dressing table

Art Nouveau designs now seemed over-elaborate and whilst simplifying her jewellery Ella also felt the need to diversify. She started a new venture in the early twenties with Kate Westrup. Kate and Emily Westrup were two unmarried sisters who came to live soon after the end of the war at Lamorna Gate, just below the turning down into the valley. Like Ella, they came from a large London family, Kate being the youngest of ten children. Emily, who did the house-keeping, was fifteen years older than her sister; Kate was only a few months older than Ella. Like Ella, she had had an artistic training and the two women had much in common. To some extent she replaced Laura as another woman artist whom she saw daily and with whom she could work. Together they started the Lamorna Pottery. It was to be another co-operative, recalling Ella's days with Partridge at Branscombe. They would share a workshop but work independently, each making her own distinctive product. Once again Colonel Paynter provided the land and the building was the usual studio of wood and corrugated iron. It was situated halfway between their two houses, just off the road at Lamorna Vean.

Ella made some delightful ceramic figures, portraits of herself and Laura Knight which stand between six and eight inches high. In one she wears a close-fitting, low-cut maroon top with a long striped skirt of maroon and grey. Her dark hair is drawn back and she holds an orange in her hand. In another she wears a long dress in a bold floral pattern; she again holds an orange and stands with one foot forward on a base of daisies. In a third she

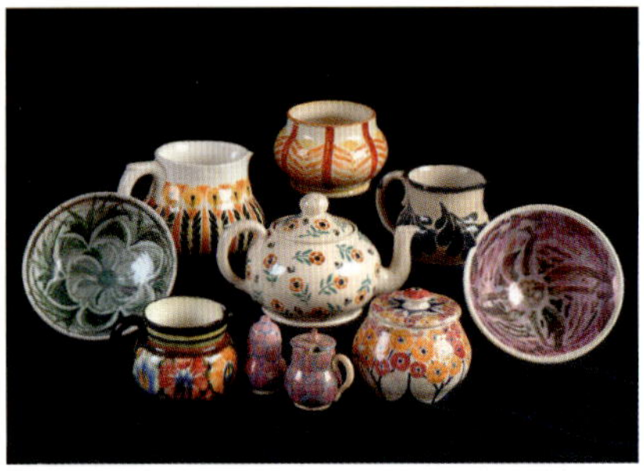

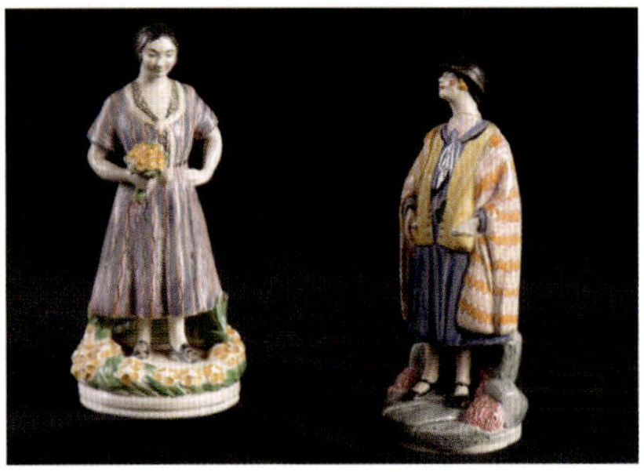

TOP
Lamorna pottery ware

Ceramic figures made by Ella of herself and Laura Knight

wears a yellow top with a black and yellow striped skirt. The other figure is larger; she stands hand on hip, wearing a pink and grey striped dress and holding a bunch of yellow flowers. The figure of Laura Knight is the same size but stouter, recognisable by her broad-brimmed black hat. She has an orange cloak over her shoulders, her hands in the pockets of a yellow cardigan. She stands four-square, as opposed to Ella's more ballet-like posture. In her self-portraits Ella knows her own attractiveness; she presents it with humour and obvious enjoyment of her own physicality.

But the pottery was a commercial venture and she needed to produce work of a more practical nature, vases, pots and jugs. Even so, she gave them something of herself, her love of colour and sensuous shape. The pots are full-bellied, the jugs squat and rounded. They are decorated with bright floral designs, usually stylised: a stalk and leaves make a herring-bone pattern in bold brush strokes with two concentric rings for the flower. The motif circles horizontally around a pot or is used vertically, curving outwards on the side of a jug. The insides of bowls are decorated with flowers and leaves in a variety of patterns and colours, the green and blue of harebells or the orange of marigolds.

Kate Westrup was a more accomplished painter than Ella. The oil on canvas of a man pitchforking manure into a cart, known as *The White Horse* as it is the horse rather than the man who dominates the picture, belonged to Ella. Kate's oil is painted with free, loose brushstrokes and stands comparison with Forbes's horses at a drinking pool or Harvey's seaweed gatherers. Ella never painted any other subject than flowers, sometimes in oil such as the delicate pink, mauve and white anemones in a glass bowl, but most often in watercolours. These are usually flowers in a vase with no background; this makes them look two-dimensional and reminiscent of Gluck's flower paintings. The delight in flowers is clear, particularly flowers from the garden: love-in-the-mist, dianthus, daisies, nasturtiums and pansies. Her watercolours were generally given away as presents. Her hand-made Christmas cards were of flowers, sometimes done in crayon.

While Ella liked to paint flowers, covering her teapots, jugs and bowls with them, Kate preferred animals, and in the pottery she specialised in animal figurines: lambs gambolling on a lawn of primroses and daisies, two black and white calves with their heads entwined, a foal under a tree in blossom, three brown and white bears, a pair of spotted hounds. They were beautifully modelled and almost, but not quite, avoided sentimentality. The pottery also produced ceramic calendars, a plaque depicting a ship in full sail or a basket of flowers from which the renewable calendar was suspended; they were very much of their period. Ella made a figure of a Newlyn fishwife stooping under the weight of a large creel or basket on her shoulders. Unlike her self-portraits these were reproduced in numbers from a mould. She had the nostalgic tourist market in mind, as the piece looks back a generation to the women painted by Walter Langley.

Ella used the contacts she had already established for her jewellery with exhibitions, shops and galleries to distribute the wares of the Lamorna Pottery. She kept the accounts and listed items that had been dispatched. In August 1926 she sent to Liverpool a jug, three jam pots, a cruet and a figurine. Kate contributed a cow and calf, ewe and lambs, goat and kids, a bull and a goat. Ella's jam pots were priced at fifteen shillings, Kate's groups at three guineas. In December she sent bowls, mugs and a figurine to the Collector's Gallery in Manchester. In the same year she showed without Kate at the Arts and Crafts Exhibition at the Royal Academy, along with such potters as Bernard Leach and Shoji Hamada. She entered a lavender pot, underglazed, which was not for sale, an overglazed pot priced at 10/- and a bowl at 7/6 (a Bernard Leach bowl was 15/-). She also entered two rings and two brooches (prices on application).

The Lamorna Pottery always exhibited at the Newlyn Gallery where in the summer of 1927 Ella sold pottery to the value of £10.8.6 and jewellery to the value of £6.19.0. She continued to make and sell jewellery throughout the period when the pottery was in operation, sending off work of both sorts to the Collector's Gallery in Manchester, the Ruslan Gallery on the Isle

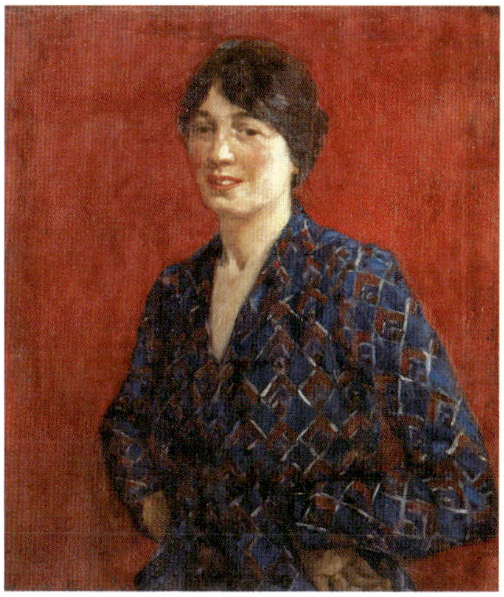

Ella Naper
Ruth Simpson
Oil on canvas, 24 x 20 in
© The Artist's Estate

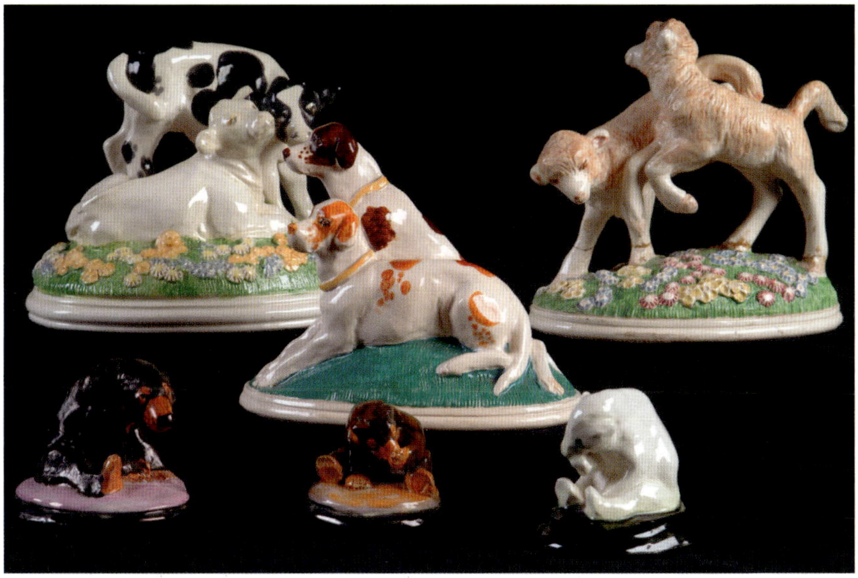

Kate Westrup: Lamorna Pottery animal figures

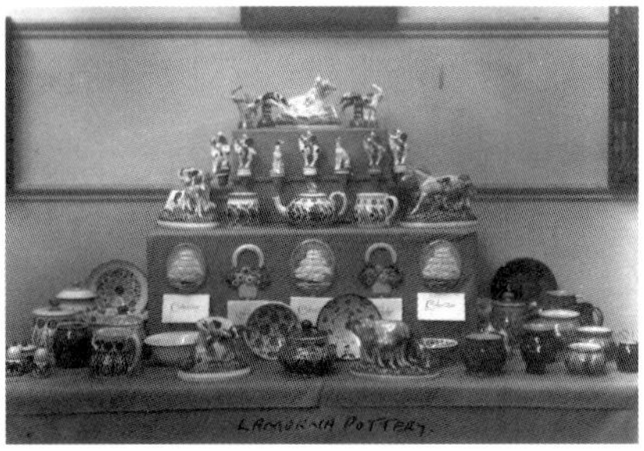

Lamorna pottery, a contemporary display at the Newlyn Gallery

of Wight and the Ruskin Museum. Heals took only jewellery, some twenty-one pieces: silver and enamelled necklaces, pendants and rings set with moonstones, pearls, agate, applegreen chrysophrase and blue chalcedony. She built up a list of clients: Lady Oppenheimer wrote wanting to see more of her work, having bought a silver and tourmaline ring that she very much admired at the Arts and Crafts exhibition.

The partnership was brought to an end by the unexpected death of Kate Westrup on 11 April 1928 at the early age of forty-three. Her elder sister Emily lived on in Lamorna until she was ninety, remaining on the lists that Ella made for Christmas gifts, mats one year, gloves another, hand-made and decorated. Lamorna Birch's grandson Adam remembers being sent up the valley at Christmas with gifts for 'the three Es': Eleanor Hughes, Ella Naper and Emily Westrup.

In Ella's accounts the last considerable dispatch of pottery was to the Isle of Wight in November 1927. After that all entries are for jewellery except for a few items with no address and no date: fishwife, teapot, two pots and a lustre bowl. They appear immediately after seven brooches and rings sent to Camberwell, undated, and six brooches sent to Newlyn in November 1929. The next entry is for twenty-one pieces of jewellery sent to Newlyn in 1930, so the last pots sold were at the end of 1929 or early in 1930. It suggests that the pottery ceased production before the end of the decade, not long after Kate Westrup's death. When Charles Simpson returned from London to Lamorna in 1931 he took it over as his studio.

Ella kept her potter's wheel until 1947 when she gave it to Chris Ludlow who started the new Lamorna Pottery in what had been the milk factory. The building at Lamorna Vean was lived in, with so many annexes added to it that it became known as Umpteen. Eventually it was pulled down and a new house built on the site.

Cornish Scarlet: Ella and Laura

CHAPTER NINE

When Laura Knight described Ella as 'an adorably lovely slim creature' her use of the word 'creature' instead of 'young woman' suggests that she saw her as instinctive and physical, with an animal vitality. Laura appreciated women's bodies with a sensuousness that could easily be misinterpreted; her description of a swimmer coming out of the water at Lamorna cove, 'the wet bathing-suit clinging close round her lovely breasts', could come straight out of an erotic novel, but her interest never went beyond the aesthetic. She had 'crushes', but she was no Gluck. With her artist's eye she adored how women looked, Ella as much as anyone.

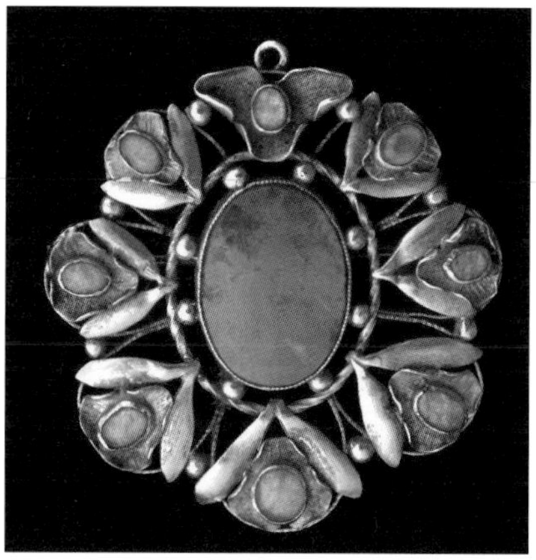

A blue and green gold pendant set with moonstones and mother of pearl

She had painted *Self and Nude* in 1913, when they had both just moved to Lamorna and lived within a few hundred yards of each other. Laura used professional models and posed them nude, dressing or undressing, on the cliffs and by the rock pools of the cove. It scandalised the village and every night the village boys came making cat-calls under the bedroom window of the cottage where they lodged. Colonel Paynter dismissed objections to their presence and built a large studio for the Knights at the bottom of Frank Heath's garden at Menwinnion. It was to this new studio rather than to the beach that Ella came to take off her clothes and pose for Laura. Even so, when the London models were regarded as no more than prostitutes, it was a very liberated thing to do.

Artist and Nude – the title varies – plays with the contrast between the clothed and naked figure. There is a power relationship between two such people, in which the clothed figure is likely to seem dominant. Laura avoids this by raising the model on a dais; Ella stands on a striped mat before an orange-red screen with her back to the artist. Laura herself is lower in the bottom left of the painting, disappearing off the canvas. She wears the cardigan of 'Cornish scarlet', as the art critic P.G. Konody christened it, that appears in many paintings and which she bought in a sale in Penzance for half-a-crown. Her wide-brimmed black hat emphasises her dressed appearance. She looks at Ella's slender figure, the pose with hands clasped behind her head revealing the full length of the body outlined against the screen. Her gaze is reflective, evaluating, workmanlike. There are three planes to the picture, the artist, the model and the canvas on which a further image of Ella appears, a painting within a painting.

At Dozmary Laura took some nude photographs of Ella. In one she stands outside the hut with the lake beyond, washing herself at a bowl on a stand. She wears a loose shift or blouse which leaves her uncovered from the waist down. In another she lies on the lakeside turf, her undulating form like low white hills rising above the grasses or like smooth boulders amongst the

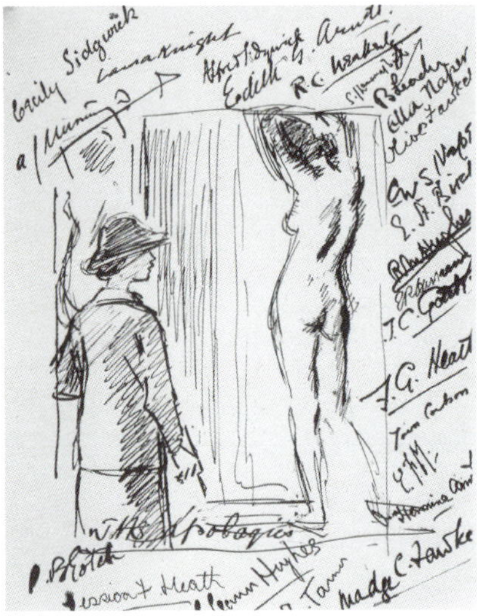

ABOVE
Parody of Self and Nude
Laura Knight, signed by other Lamorna artists.
Reproduced with permission of the Estate of Gilbert Evans and Curtis Brown Group Ltd, London on behalf of the Estate of Dame Laura Knight.
© Dame Laura Knight

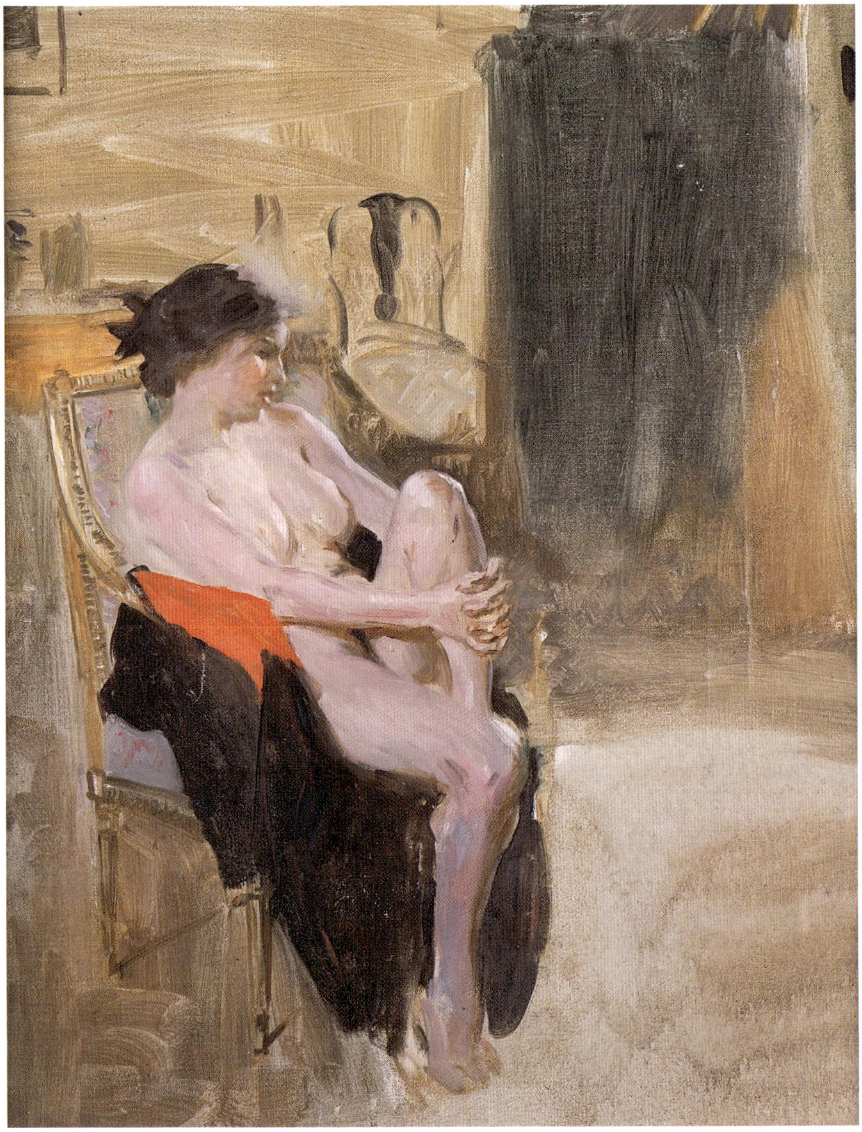

Ella, Nude in Chair
Laura Knight
Oil on canvas, 29 x 22 in
Reproduced with permission of Curtis Brown Group Ltd, London on behalf of the Estate of Dame Laura Knight.
© Dame Laura Knight

OPPOSITE
Self and Nude 1913
Laura Knight
Reproduced with permission of Curtis Brown Group Ltd, London on behalf of the Estate of Dame Laura Knight.
Copyright © Dame Laura Knight.
In the collection of the National Portrait Gallery, London

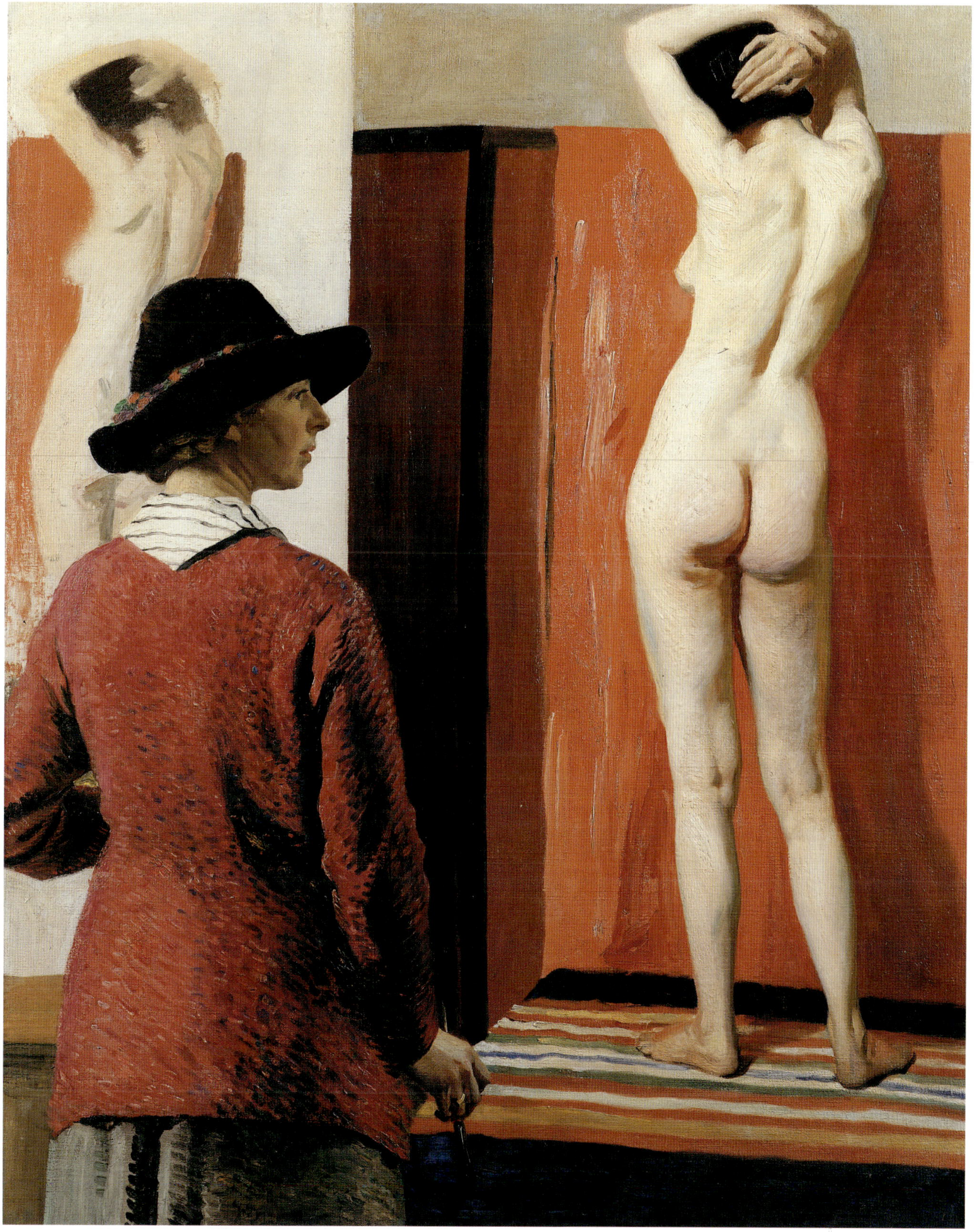

sedge. Only one of these photographs is of its period: Ella kneels in flimsy drapery in a pose reminiscent of Isadora Duncan. This may have been set up by Harold as he used the photo of Ella for the figure in his 1916 Royal Academy exhibit *Dozmare Pool*, his sketches of the lake beneath huge skies providing the background. It is skilfully painted, but the symbolism of the figure is less attractive than Laura's immediate response. Harold Knight also painted Ella as a nude on the rocks of Lamorna Cove. His working method was far less spontaneous than Laura's; he was likely to have built up his painting from studies made of Ella in the studio and sketches done on the beach. Laura was true to what she saw before her.

From their first meeting as neighbours in 1913 the two women remained friends for the rest of their lives. Ella taught Laura enamelling and they worked together in the studio at Trewoofe. Laura had been enthralled by the Russian Ballet in London the previous year and saw every performance of Pavlova and Karsavina, making notes from the stalls; this was her inspiration for the enamels she produced with Ella. A beautiful pendant survives from this partnership: Laura's enamelled ballet dancer is in a setting made by Ella, and it is signed EN & LK 1915 (see page 83).

When Harold and Laura left Cornwall, they all kept in touch, the Knights returning each summer and when Ella and Charles visited London they always stayed with them in St John's Wood, at 9 Langford Place (later re-numbered 16). Ella and Laura wrote to each other, sent Christmas cards and exchanged gifts. Laura's letters are deeply affectionate, even allowing

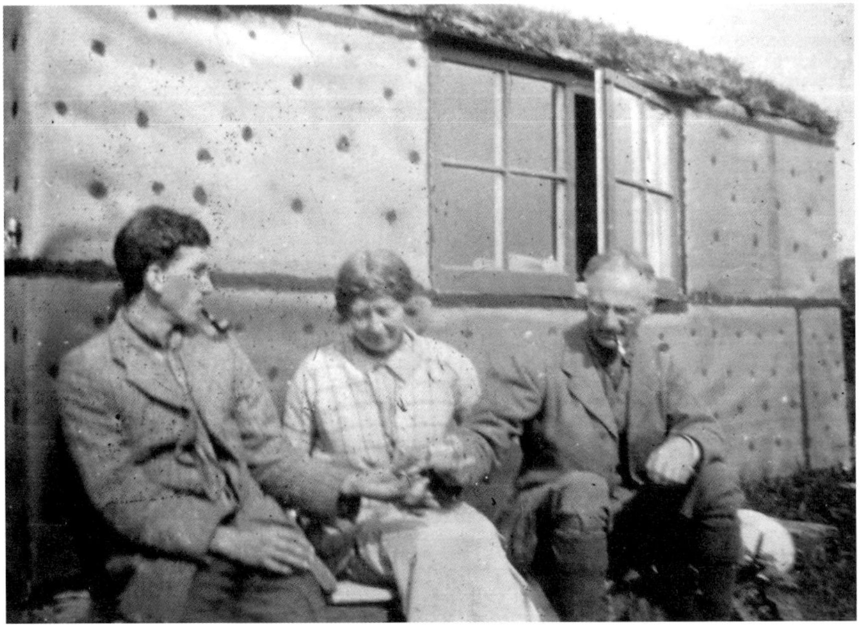

Dozmary: Charlie with Laura and Harold Knight

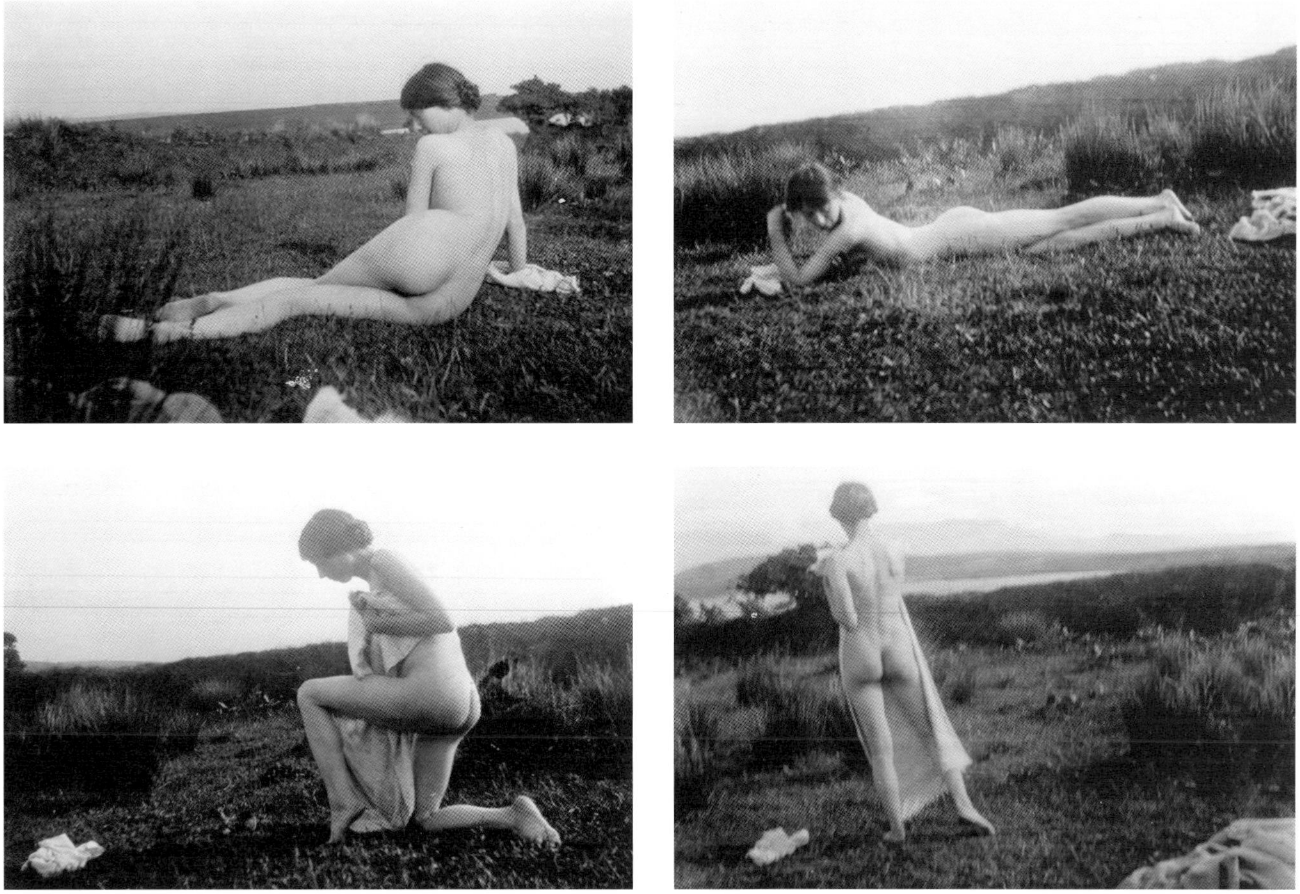

Laura's photographs of Ella nude at Dozmary

for her normal effusiveness. They were usually written in haste; as she became well-known she was always busy with paintings, exhibitions and correspondence. In one letter she says that she has spent the whole day correcting the proofs of her autobiography, 'a most awfully trying job'; she then went on to write fifteen letters 'but couldn't put the pen down to say how often we think of you and how much we love you'. Her letters are addressed to her 'Dearest Friends' or her 'Beloved Friends'; sometimes they are simply to 'My dearest Ella'. Charles is always remembered, usually at the end. Laura writes in the first person plural but there is little about Harold, mostly that he has flu, is not feeling well but is working hard, has been knocked down by a car.

There are lots of thank-yous, not only for Ella's beautiful letters but for the gifts she has sent. These were often a reminder of the Lamorna that Laura missed so much. Ella and Charles sent a grey mullet up to Langford Place. 'You are darlings to send it – we baked it in butter – it was perfect.' They sent Cornish cream which could not be obtained in London. Ella sent

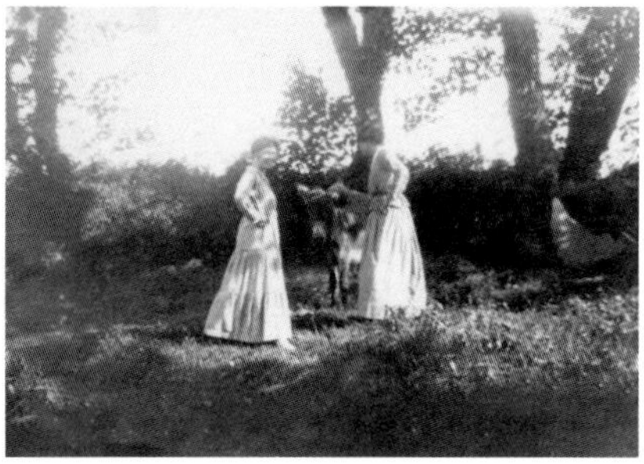

Ella and Laura Knight at Trewoofe

flowers from the garden at Trewoofe, a nosegay of early blooms and the primroses that Laura always loved and which made her so nostalgic for Cornwall. Also from the garden came a bunch of herbs, which Laura hung by her bed.

She sent presents that she had made, jewellery or pottery. Ella gave Laura a ring and earrings: 'I adore them and adore wearing them, not only for their beauty but because you made them.' She sent dishes 'which arrived most perfectly without a crack' and a jumper: 'I love it and you are a brick to give it to me.' She sent material for curtains, 'which will look so rich', not meaning sumptuous but always Laura's word of approval. 'I have not had time to make them yet but will do so this week.'

Ella loved materials in bright colours and bold designs, and with Laura and Phyllis Yglesias hunted them out in shops in Penzance and London. She bought clothes from Crysćde, the colourful silks designed by Alec Walker and produced in Newlyn. She and Laura made dresses for themselves, sometimes using furnishing material if the pattern was striking. One of A.J. Munning's party-pieces was a song about Ella and Laura vying with others for the most impressive frocks. There was even a poem inspired by Ella's underwear. Her bookcase contained a slim volume of poetry entitled *The Lovers and Other Poems* and inside was a folded sheet of paper with some typed verses:

PIMPERNEL

My true love wears
For her own delight
Gay little breeches
Of Silks so bright –
The gallantest colours
That gold can buy
For slender hip
And rounded thigh.

There on the hearth rug
She squats herself,
A wicked industrious
Tailor-wise elf,
And swift is the needle
And elf-like the stitches

That go for to make her
Her little bright breeches.

Amethyst, emerald,
Speedwell-blue,
Buttercup, poppy
And amber too,
Turquoise and topaz
And tangerine,
Purple, vermillion,
Ultramarine,
Apple green, grass green,
Sea green, jade –
Every colour and
Every shade,
Shimmering-shining
Out of sight
She wears them all
For her own delight.

Gravely she goes
As she deems it meet,
Stepping sedately
Down the street,
And I laugh to myself
For I know so well
She is wearing her breeches
Of pimpernel.

Was it really written for Ella? It is very smooth and professional, in style like the entertainments that A.P. Herbert wrote for *Punch* in the twenties. It could have been copied from a publication, but either way it is a very convincing picture of her: the slender hips, the industrious needle, the colours of flowers and precious stones, the love of bright clothes. But who could have been so cheeky? The chief suspect must be Gluck, who wrote poetry, light verses mostly, throughout her life and who was capable of writing in old age a poem beginning 'I've had 'em all / The short and tall'. *Pimpernel* was tucked into the book of love poems, just the sort of present that Gluck might have given Ella.

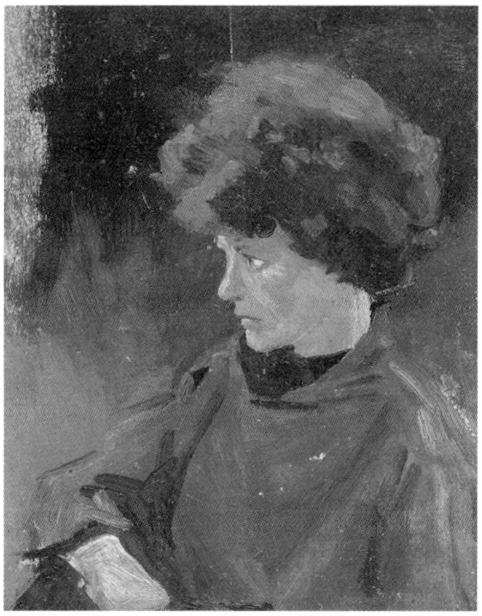

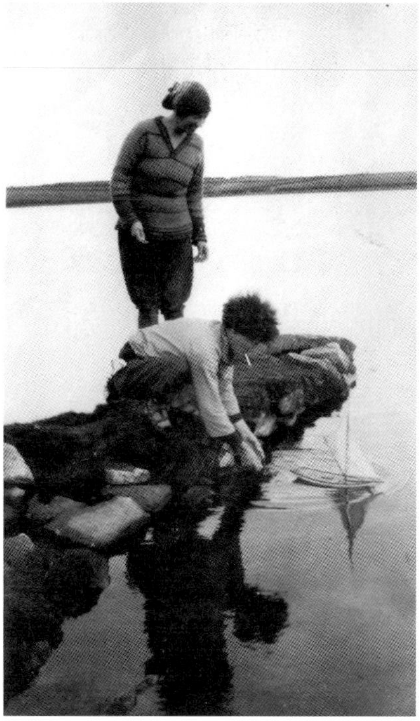

TOP
'Golly' (Phyllis Yglesias)
Charles Naper
Oil on board, 6 x 5 in

Ella and 'Golly' at Dozmary

Laura and Ella gave and lent each other clothes and materials. Laura lends her 'Beloved Ella' a Russian dress and a little jacket to wear with it: 'Wear them as much as you want to… How grand it is that you are going to have a bit of a do!' Ella posts to Laura some old sheets. 'Ella dear, I have cut 9 pillow slips out of the 2 poorer sheets and have made up 3 or 4 lav cloths out of the scraps and still have some left for tea cloths – the 2 other sheets can be mended to wear.' Laura ordered some 'knitted things' for Ella and then realised the bill for £1.18.0 would be enclosed so sent a cheque for £2 to cover it.

As well as clothes they are interested in décor, and Laura describes what she has done to the house. 'I have painted the staircase black and it looks so nice and have been trying to get the old varnish stain off the doors preparatory to staining and can't remember the stain Charlie told me of.' A little later, 'I painted the arches white and the columns a matt black and they look wonderfully fine then the staircase has been done black and the hall floor all the varnish taken off (which was some job) and stained and the mantelpiece that Charlie boxed painted and decorated.'

They wrote to each other about their work. 'I am aquatinting again, I often want my Ella by me to help handle the metals – working on steel and iron – great fun, just done a large life-size head of Miriam and can't help feeling a little bucked with it… it is such a wonderful medium when you get used to it. I want to do some very big plates now but it means getting such big acid baths it is a nuisance, however I shall have to manage it somehow otherwise I can't rest. I think the older I get the more I am inclined to black and white so long as you can get a beautiful medium to do it in… I am just going through one of my mad enthusiastic stages.' Ella sent her a press in reply. 'Ever so many thanks for the press it arrived in perfect condition and I have already put it together and learnt all about it from a book – now am longing to start making some messes. It takes quite a good sized plate, I am delighted with it.'

Ella was unfortunate with her London agents and galleries. The Miriam whose full-sized head Laura had done in aquatint treated her badly in some way, and Laura was filled with rage. 'I expect you will have heard that I have busted up with Miriam.' She moved to a different gallery, but if Ella still wanted flowered material from Miriam, Laura could get it from her without letting her know who it was for. 'I want her to realise how rotten she has been to you.' Ella had another bad experience with a London agent and Harold wrote: 'We have not yet got over the blow of Jan Plichta's incompetence, but I suppose nothing can be done. I should certainly take all the other things out of his hands as soon as possible, and let him know that you are not satisfied with his efforts.'

Ella supplied news of the Knights' friends in Lamorna. Laura always wanted to know how they were. She was always thinking of Cornwall, hoping they could come down, wishing that Ella and Charlie would come and stay. When Harold was in America in 1926 and she was sailing to join him, she wanted them to stay in Langford Place. 'I hope it might have been a change for you.' She wrote to Ella from mid-Atlantic. It had been a rough crossing: 'some spectacle a big storm in mid-ocean! A grand piano stood on end and port-holes were burst and people injured.' But Laura was not sea-sick. 'I was never hungrier and found it all most thrilling.' After America, 'we are really and truly coming to Cornwall on Friday or Sat and are going to Ber's first, we would love to come to you for a few days later if we may. I am so excited about it I don't know what to do, it's so rich to think of seeing you all again in your own nests in the country and the SEA.'

Ber, or Bernard Walke, was the unconventional vicar of St Hilary near Penzance, married to the artist Annie Walke and author of *Twenty Years at St Hilary*. He was nationally known for the Christmas plays performed in his church and broadcast direct each year by the BBC. Later Bernard stayed with Harold and Laura at Langford Place, and Laura wrote to Ella that 'he left yesterday taking with him a lovely old 14 century wood (French) figure for the church. He wants a big crucifix for about £50, of course could not get anything with any artistic merit at all. Harold and I suggested Gol should do him one in her different coloured woods. It would be a fine chance for her to do a big thing like that, I am sure she could make a wonderful thing of it. If you see her, make her do it, as Ber is crazy that she should and he has the funds put by. Thank you so much for sending the saucepans.' Phyllis Yglesias, also known as Golly or Pog, was exhibiting sculptured panels in woods of different colours at Foyles' Gallery in London. She made the crucifix for St Hilary church, a powerful and moving piece.

Laura's letters frequently give amusing accounts of small disasters or awkwardnesses. She was given a puppy who could not be house-trained, even though Harold walked it up and down for hours. 'We were awash,' she wrote. The dog had to go. 'It was a pity because she was a little gem of a Cairn and apart from her incontinence was perfect.'

But sometimes she spoke straight from the heart and just wanted Ella's sympathy. She broke her leg again, as she had once before in the Napers' paddock when Ella was in London. She hated being a burden and helpless, her privacy lost 'under the hand of a competent nurse who has wiped thousands of people's bottoms and I am just one of them.' She consoled herself with thoughts of Cornwall. 'Are the primroses out on the steps? Dear Trewoofe, I can see it so plainly.'

The letters that Laura Knight wrote to Ella between the wars are full of longing, of longing for Cornwall and Lamorna and Trewoofe and her own dear dear Ella.

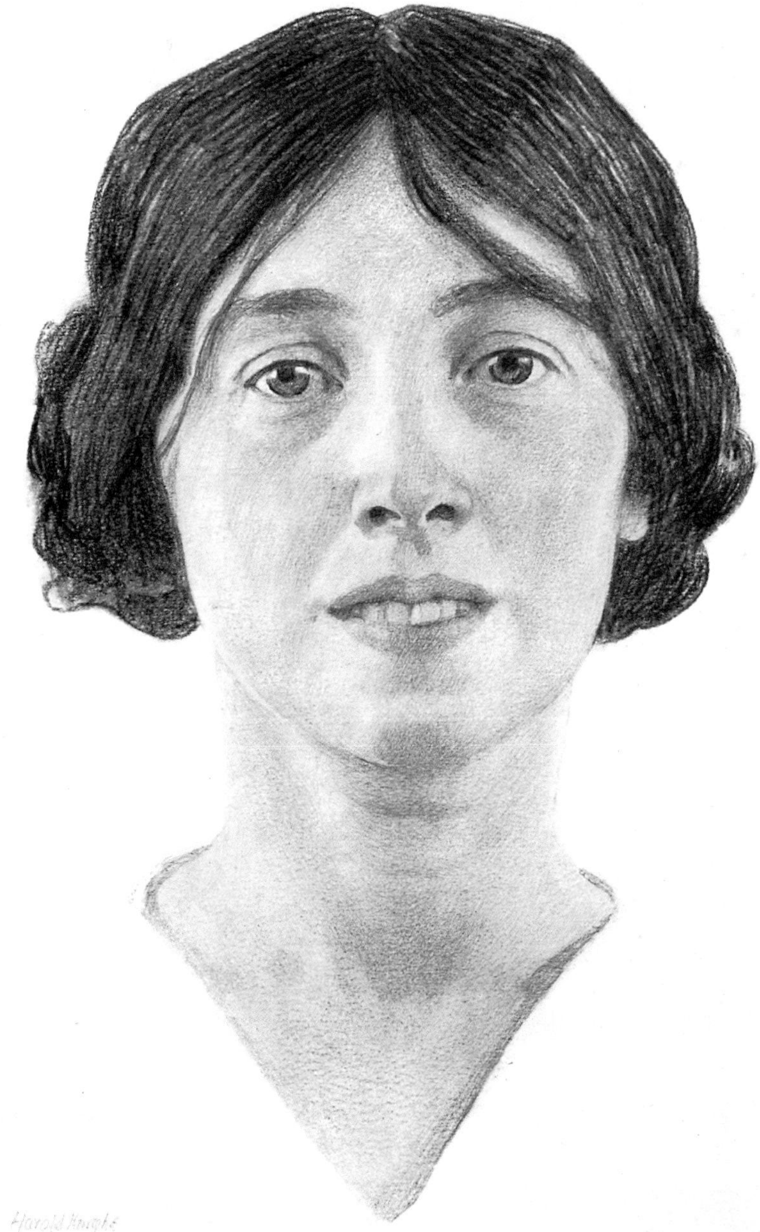

Ella Naper, head of
Harold Knight
Pencil drawing
Reproduced with permission
of Curtis Brown Group Ltd, London
on behalf of the Estate of Harold Knight.
© Harold Knight

Silver: The Middle Years

CHAPTER TEN

Life for Ella and Charles in the thirties was not as financially constrained as before. They had a car and planned an extended visit to Scotland, influenced by John Birch's praise of the country. Birch travelled north to spend months in the castles and houses of rich clients who bought his paintings of the surrounding landscape.

He sometimes wrote to Ella, dashing off a page or two in his tiny almost illegible handwriting as though he were continuing a conversation begun the day before. Outwardly he gave every appearance of relishing the life of the rich, with their Rolls-Royce cars and sporting estates in Scotland, and seemed perfectly at ease in their society, but underneath he felt 'edgy'. From Selkirk he decides 'to tip Ella a line' as he has a few minutes to spare, and says how much he loves the country with its hills and rivers, 'tho I am not greatly excited staying in a big house where everything goes so much by clockwork... I never was made for the life of a countyman... I wouldn't leave any little muddy hut for a lot. I simply can't bear being kept to dance – which was truly made for slaves.' Although he's about to be taken out 'in a big beautiful car I'd rather have a fishing rod and sketch book and creep away up the dales... To be taken about in luxury is not conducive to painting... But you know the feeling Ella? When the world offers you everything you don't want it.'

But Ella and Charlie had not yet had the chance to see Scotland, knowing of it mainly from Birch's paintings of mountains and rivers and his stories of fishing for trout and salmon. It appealed to Charlie, who never showed any interest in his ancestral home in Ireland, and at nine o'clock on the morning of 12 June 1934 they set out on their tour of Lamorna Birch's Scotland. They had a list of recommended bed and breakfast establishments and on the first day they completed two hundred and fourteen miles, spending the night in the Cotswolds. From then on the diary, which Ella must have written up entirely for the benefit of Charles, contains nothing but stopping places, mileages and fuel consumption. They travelled through Leicester and York to Edinburgh, buying four gallons of Shell at Lairg for six shillings. They visited all the places familiar to Birch: Selkirk, Inverness, Lochinver. At Lochinver a picture postcard of Penzance was waiting *poste restante* for Ella. It was unsigned, but the parody of holiday advertising could only have come from Alfred Sidgwick: 'As you are still on your travels you might have a look at this place some day. Excellent accommodation to be had at Trewoofe, in a charming house standing in its own grounds which include a lake providing trout for breakfast. Fresh eggs and clotted cream from the home farm. Many interesting prehistoric remains in the neighbourhood and specially one literary couple.'

When they had been away a month they started to return by way of the Lake District and then headed south east, to be in Berkshire for the first birthday of Nell's daughter Maryella. They visited Ella's parents, now living in Bromley, Kent, leaving on 19 July at 7.20 a.m. and reaching home eight hours later.

Just before setting out on their Scottish holiday, Ella had had a strange little tiff with Aunt Cis about international politics. Cecily Sidgwick wrote to her immediately: 'Dearest One, I can't sleep without telling you how sorry I am I said a word about communism today. I don't care about that kind of politics now. It's dead I think. You seem to me to have altered a great deal since I first knew you. In the early days you were all for Harold, GBS and Co. [Harold Laski, the influential Marxist writer and theorist, at this time Professor of Political Science at the London School of Economics and George Bernard Shaw, the essayist and playwright, co-founder of the Fabian Society.] I really can't write about it. I don't think anything about you today except what is affectionate and grateful for all your sweetness to us. Yours ever, Cis.'

It is difficult to imagine what caused Ella to flare up. She had socialist convictions in her youth; it was part of the ethos of the Schools of Arts and Crafts, and she shared the beliefs of her sister Marion and her partner Hubert. If she had changed as Mrs Sidgwick thought, then it could only be that as she grew older and slightly more affluent she had modified her views while Mrs Sidgy, like many left-wing intellectuals in the thirties still held fast to Communist ideals – not a view that the Dornford Yates world of her novels confirms. Perhaps Aunt Cis had made a remark about motor cars and Scottish tours which touched a raw nerve, making Ella feel as Birch did, something of a traitor to her class and beliefs.

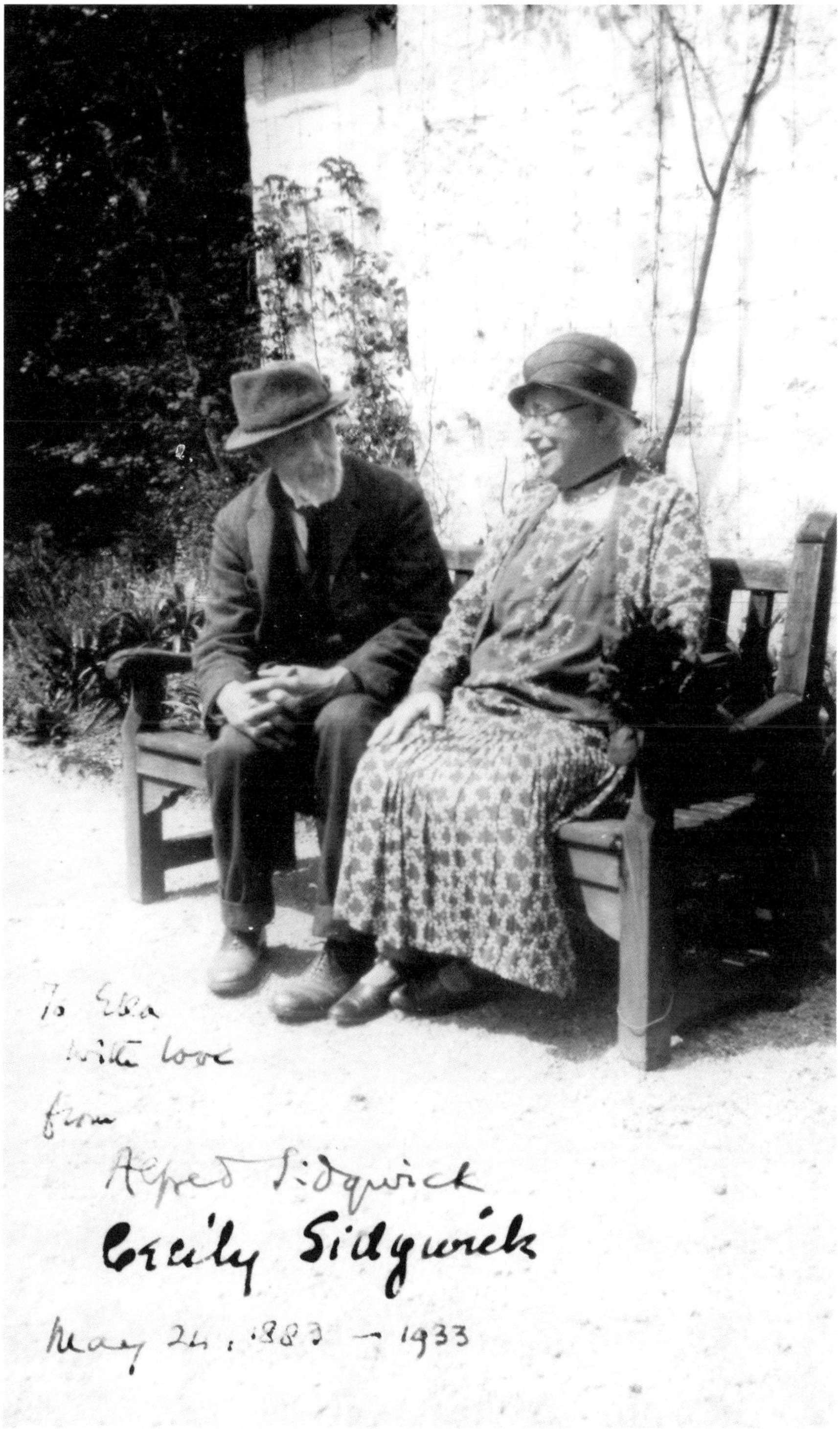

Alfred and Cecily Sidgwick
on their Golden Wedding

Not long after their return from Scotland Aunt Cis was taken ill and died within two days, on 10 August 1934. She left a letter for Alfred: 'Goodbye. Don't be unhappy… Ella, the darling, will look after you, but let her off the funeral.' Ella nevertheless went to the service in St Buryan church. Cecily had been seriously ill three years earlier and had then given detailed instructions for the burial and other arrangements. She wanted Ella to have her wrist-watch, fur coat and boa and silver toilet set, Laura Knight to have her golden Italian beads. 'Dear Mrs Sidgy!' wrote Laura to Ella, 'I think of all the great kindnesses that she did us, her hospitality and friendship… I feel so sad that she is gone, dear soul.' When Ella forwarded the necklace, she wrote back that somehow it made her feel 'the meanest skunk alive'.

'Poor Mr Sidgy!' she wrote, 'I feel so grieved for him.' He had his eighty-fourth birthday a week after the funeral and then set out on a sentimental journey. 'Uncle A to Bristol,' notes Ella in her diary, but in fact she had been deeply involved in the preparations. He was going to visit relatives in Bristol and Liverpool, then go on to the Lake District which had memories for him and finally to Skipton in Yorkshire where he had been born and grew up. He was travelling alone by train; Ella saw him to Penzance station and insisted that he went first class.

From Bristol he wrote the first of almost daily letters to Ella, thousands of words written in a tiny but very legible script flowing evenly on the page. His wife, whom he loved dearly, had died, he is on a journey which he thinks will be his last and that he has not long to live; freed from all restraint he tells Ella how much he loves her. They are not the letters of an old man in his dotage; they are clever, amusing, honest. Ella would have looked forward to the arrival of the postman at Trewoofe.

As soon as he arrives in Bristol he writes describing the journey, making it personal to her by thinking of the area around Liskeard as 'her' country, the line to Looe as 'her' railway. He is staying in Clifton where his grandfather on his mother's side had once had a house. The guests at dinner were the Vice-Chancellor of the University and his wife, 'the former quite interesting as he knew a good deal of the philosophical world. But Mrs Loveday was too severe for my taste, though forgivable because she is a Yorkshirewoman.' Loveday was catching a train to London at seven the next morning, returning at lunchtime for two meetings in the afternoon. It made Alfred feel quite dizzy. 'Give me a quiet game of chess at Trewoofe Orchard,' he writes, 'and wireless music in the evening.' But Clifton is an interesting neighbourhood and 'I do wish you and I could see it together.' He says that in a sense she is with him all the time.

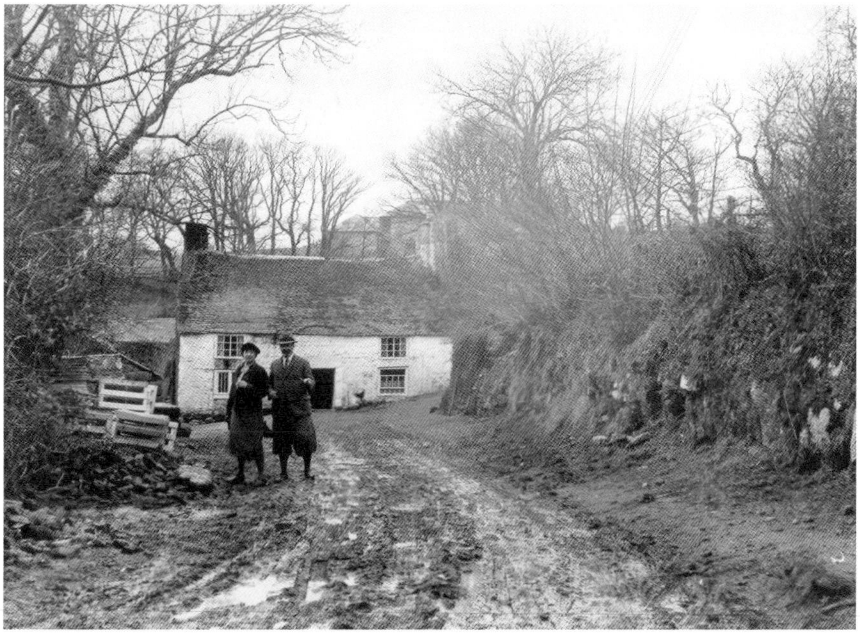

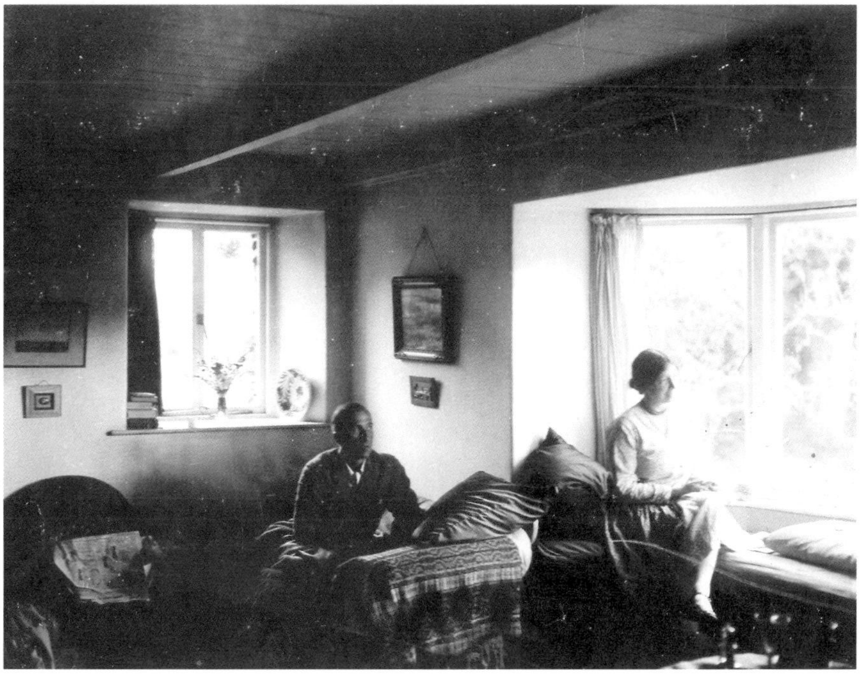

LEFT
Ella with S. J. Lamorna Birch outside Trewoofe Farm

Ella and Charlie in the sitting room of Trewoofe

He prefers to avoid conventional beginnings and endings to letters. 'Hooray I have escaped,' he begins as he leaves Bristol. He has not liked the people he met there. A relative he has known since a boy is now in business: 'his opinions have a definitional finality that I hope mine will never have.' He has a keen eye for people and places.

In Woolworth's in Liverpool he buys two of Cecily's books for Ella. 'So your extravagant uncle who travels first class for his own comfort thinks 1/-

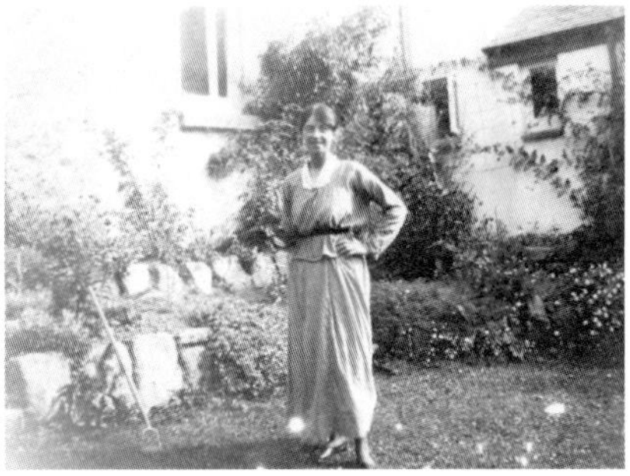

TOP
Ella in the garden at Trewoofe c.1914

Ella and Charlie outside Trewoofe c.1914

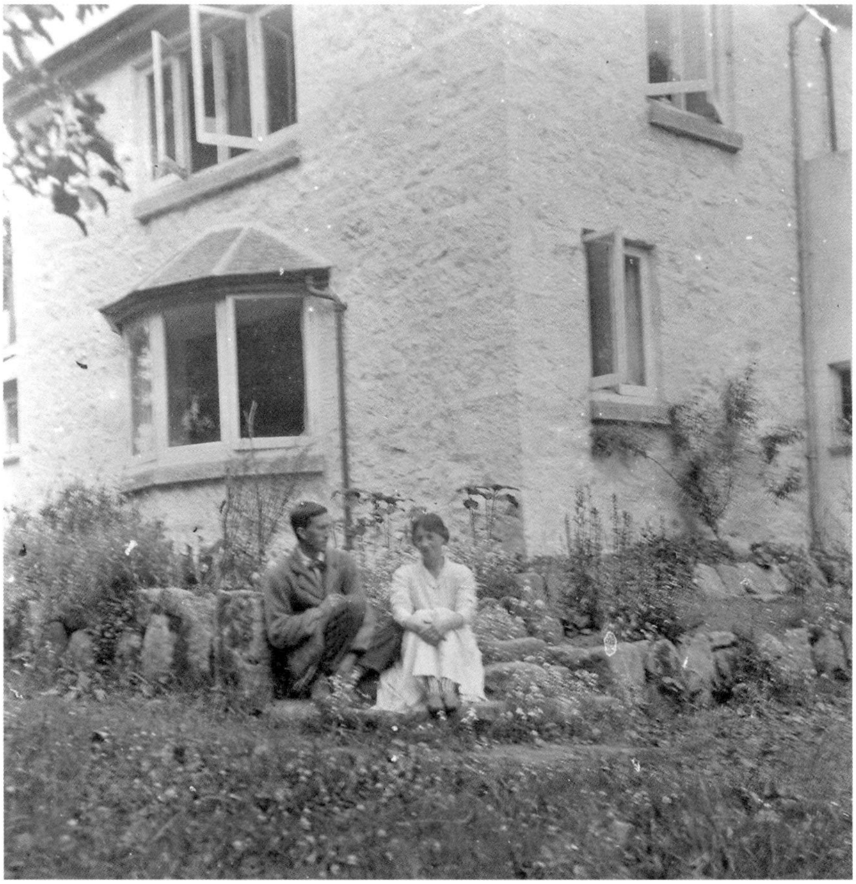

enough to spend as a present for his dearest niece.' He mentions travelling the next stage third class in order to economise, but Ella writes back so firmly that he replies, 'All right, I obey orders, Mother dear.' With a touch of understandable vanity, he asks her to check the post at Trewoofe Orchard and see if two magazines have arrived, one being *Mind* and the other *Analysis*. He has articles in both. He signs off as 'your affectionate friend and uncle and child and more'.

His next letters were sent to Ella at the Cades at The Minack House, where she was spending a week with her friend Dorothy, always known as Dofferty though later she was generally known as Rowena Cade, the creator of the Minack theatre. Alfred is glad that she is having a holiday from housework and he sends them all oatcakes. Charles was left to look after himself.

He wonders if they have read the report of Augustus John's son falling from the cliffs at Newquay. He recalls meeting John in Lamorna before Ella's time: 'a cross between a pirate chief and Jesus Christ – in looks, I mean'. He is disturbed to hear about the oil in the sea off Porthcurno. In further letters he describes Ambleside and Skipton, where he visits the old family home.

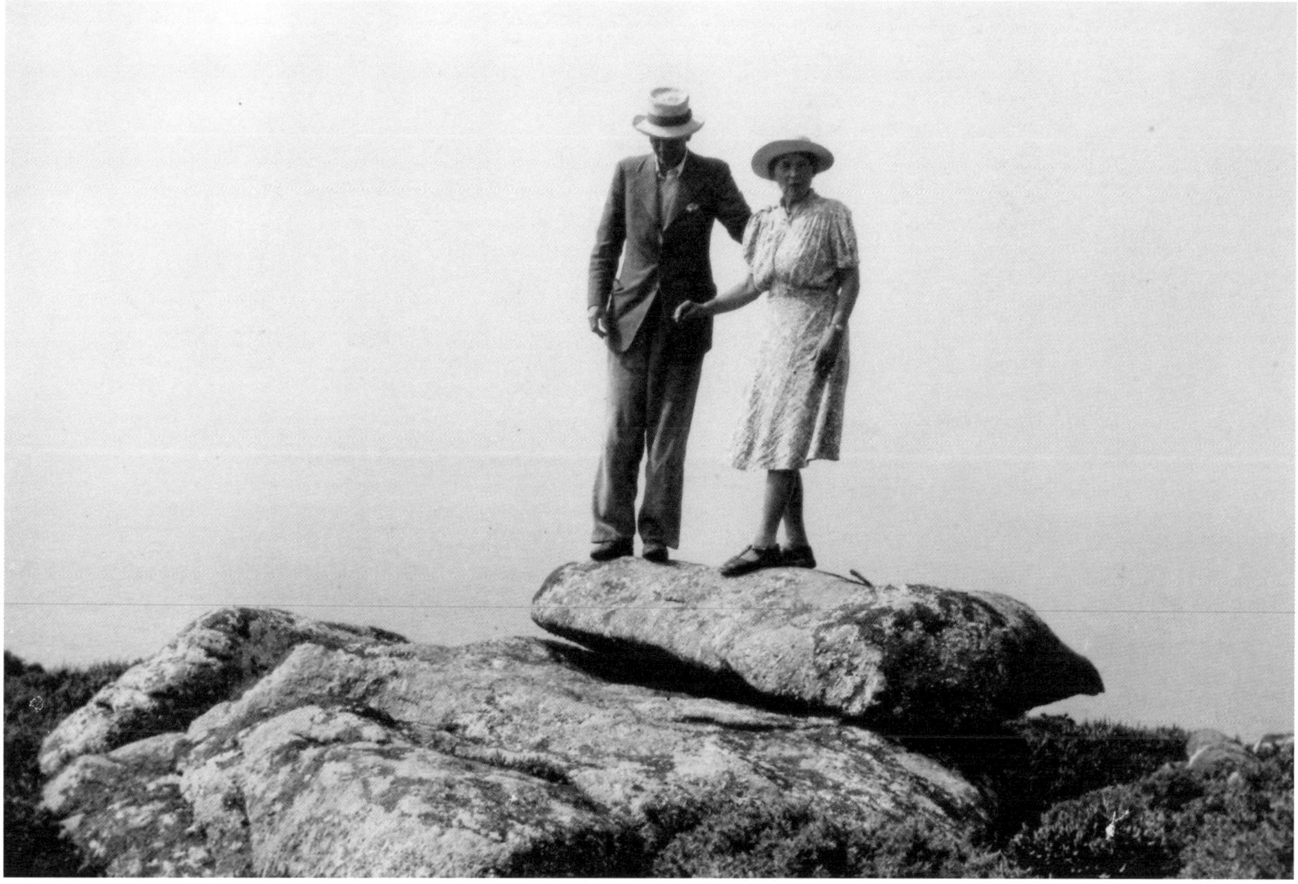

Ella and Charlie in the 1930s

New houses have been built all around it and he feels all the sadness and nostalgia of such visits. He conveys a sense of 'last time' about the places he goes to. He is longing now to get home 'and perhaps have some games of chess with you'. He had taught Ella to play chess when she had stayed at Trewoofe Orchard during the war, and when she won a game it was an important enough occasion to enter in her diary; along with 'sowed sweet peas' and 'tilled garlic', 'checkmated Uncle A' appeared three times that year. She checkmated Charlie once.

When he has a letter from Ella he is so glad, though he wishes it were she who had come instead. 'Lying awake last night I thought of all sorts of things I wanted to say to you and now of course they have gone from my old mind. Perhaps some of them could not be put down on paper anyhow.'

On his return he wrote another letter: 'Ella dear, I know you couldn't bear to talk about post-mortem money affairs, and so I am writing this for you to read after I die. Cecy and I often thought about the pity it was that you couldn't have a servant so as to get your time more free.' They had made codicils to their wills, each leaving £1,000 to her after their deaths.

He explains his exact financial situation and says that he would like to increase the amount some day. 'Even so, it can never nearly equal all that I owe to you.' In March of the next year he adds another £1,300 to the codicil. 'So now it will be as if you had won the *Daily Mail* crossword puzzle that you and I so vainly tried for.' In fact, Professor Sidgwick lived on for another nine years.

Lamorna Birch too wished that Ella could come into money. He writes from Fort William in the same year; before going north he had seen Harold Knight who had been left £12,000 by an aunt. 'He tells me it makes him feel easier, as he and Laura never had much of a gift in the way of saving… Ella my dear, I can only wish an old aunt would leave you £12,000. Even £10,000 would do.' He asks Ella to keep the news to herself. 'Entre nous' is an expression that crops up more than once in his letters. He had seen Gluck and Craig in London, when Gluck was working on one of her paintings of boxers, 'frightfully serious too. Am I rude or isn't it the proper time to laugh? Anyway don't you laugh – as this is entre nous!' On his return from Australia he rushed through the Royal Academy. 'Laura's pictures I simply can't bear – entre nous.' He thought her colours too bright, and Dod Procter's paintings he detested. He liked Ella because, as a jeweller, she was no challenge to him, and he could speak freely to her. A dance at the Faull's was amusing, 'tho I couldn't help but wish there were a few more artistic souls there – a lot of the Hunting fraternity whose minds I often think are on a par with the foxes they hunt'.

After many years painting out of doors in all weathers and standing in streams and rivers to fish, Birch suffered from rheumatism. Ella advised him to take turpentine, which sounds dangerous but he tried it and it worked. He writes to Ella, realising it is odd to send a letter when she is just up the road, to say that he is heaps better and that 'a turp in time saves nine'. He swallowed a spoonful – 'I fairly fizzed afterwards' – and combined it with rubbing externally; his legs are functioning, his shoulder easier. 'I could have cried with thankfulness… What a joy! I feel I have never love enough – all those dear ones who gave me so much of their sympathy and kindness, you, dear thing, above all.'

When Ella is unwell he writes from Flagstaff Cottage to say: 'What an awful woman you are to get knocked up just when we are all ready for our beano – I had so looked forward to seeing you and telling you about my adventures in Newcastle – I'm nearly through with a picture of a snowy river. The South Tyne and what a lovely river it is. It is near the old Roman Wall at a place called Haltwhistle and I am most excited about it.'

He writes from a hotel in Rothiemay to say that 'the river is one of my heart's desires' but that the people are 'deathly dull… I'm painting a lot in self-defence. I went fishing yesterday with a parson… a very nice man, but then you know Ella, a parson and your humble servant do not make very exciting companionship'. He is going to have lunch with a man whom he describes as 'a lad and I wish you knew him. He can far outshine me in the [art?] of paying compliments to the "fair". Now you'll say I'm being chatty so I'd better stop. Be kind then and forgive my rambling. I can't tell you all my thoughts, how much I love you or anything like that, you'd just laugh, so I must perforce be mundane and say just the kind things of life.'

Three very different men have said the same thing in almost identical words in their letters, that they feel more for Ella than it would be prudent to write: Harold Knight who fell hopelessly in love with her, Alfred Sidgwick who saw in her all that was young, vital and beautiful and felt towards her as a father, friend 'and more', and Lamorna Birch, who probably said more than he really felt. Artistic communities are usually lavish with their endearments, and Birch enjoyed the company of younger attractive women and flirting with them. It is always 'a thousand thanks', and 'what a delightful wonderful person you are' (for mending an unnamed object), 'bye-bye, my lovely'. But clearly he was fond of Ella. Charles is almost non-existent in the letters of all three men; Birch occasionally adds at the end 'Salaams to Charlie'.

On the last day of 1933 Birch wrote to say that he had had tea with Uncle Alfred, who told him that Ella's father was unwell. 'I had no idea when you were with us of how ill your father was… please give him my best remembrances and say I have never forgotten him.' He recovered partially, and Ella stayed for a week each January in Bromley, whilst in London buying a Jaeger coat which would have suited her rather better than Aunt Cis's fur coat and boa. Alfred Champion died on Easter Day 1935; Ella recorded simply in her diary 'Dad went'. A few days later she travelled to Bromley for the funeral and on her return planted Aunt Cis's grave, before getting flu.

One other death shocked them all that year. On 6 October Ernest and Dod Procter came to supper at Trewoofe to say farewell. He had just been appointed Director of Studies in Design and Craft at the Glasgow School of Art and they were leaving Newlyn. Two weeks later he was dead. Birch wrote to Ella from Inverness: 'What a shock to read in the paper of the death of Ernest Procter. What an awful thing… Two nights before we left home he and Dod came to see us and we wished each other luck!!!' 'Poor Dod,' wrote Laura Knight. 'I hope that she is getting reconciled and that she can stay in Cornwall… she hates London.'

Earlier that year was the twenty-fifth anniversary of Ella and Charlie's marriage and they celebrated their silver wedding jointly with Bertie and Eleanor Hughes who had also married in 1910. They had supper together at Chyangwheal. If Ella looked back on those twenty-five years, she had cause to be satisfied. She had known the sadness that most people experience in mid-life, as parents and older friends die, but she had known love and friendship. They had been happy and productive years. There are some three hundred and fifty recorded pieces of jewellery, not counting that produced at Branscombe and Great Tree, the busiest and most creative period of her life, and she did not always record everything. She must have made at least five hundred, possibly a thousand pieces of jewellery, all of them well-crafted and some of superb quality. She had run a pottery and with Charlie made a beautiful home and garden.

She always did everything herself; it was part of her outlook on life. When Uncle Alfred wished she could have a servant to give her more free time, it was not simply a matter of not being able to afford it; domestic help was very cheap in the twenties and thirties. She did not want someone to wait on her. It was partly a matter of principle, partly convenience as servants could be more trouble than they were worth if Mrs Sidgwick's novels are to be believed. And Charles did not like people in the house anyway.

She rolled her own cigarettes, she baked her own bread; her Chelsea buns were especially good. Janet Dunbar interviewed Ella when she was writing her life of Laura Knight and recalled her delicious omelette made with fresh herbs from the garden. When Charlie's brother Lenox came to lunch with his wife Daphne, it was 'one of the best we've ever had'. If Ella writes in her diary 'swept chimney' it means that she did it with her own hands, not that the sweep came. She was seen in her eighties standing on the kitchen table distempering the ceiling.

If she had no children, she had nieces and nephews in whom she could take an interest. In August 1935 Nell, her husband Jack and their two children stayed at Porthcurno. They went to St Ives together, had tea with the Birches and Ella entertained Maryella on her own one day. At the end of three weeks she went back with them, stopping off in Dorchester to find the Naper's Mite Almshouses in South Street and sending Charlie a picture postcard with a cross to mark the building founded in 1646 by Sir William Naper. She spent a week in Bromley before returning to Cornwall with her brother Alex and his wife Edie. They too had no children; one day they made a foursome with John Birch and visited St Ives, another evening they

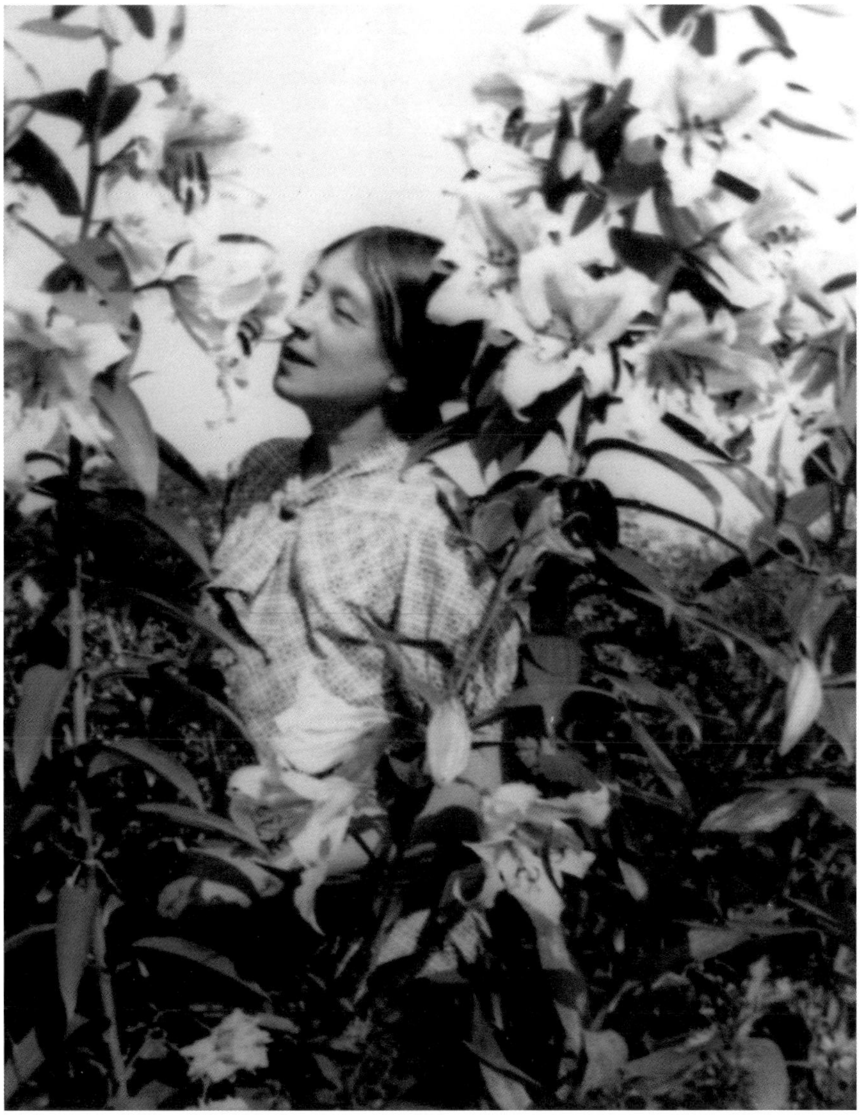

Ella in her garden

went to the pictures in Penzance. Ella enjoyed films, a liking she shared with Uncle Alfred. They liked the shots of wild animals in Tarzan films and they both thought that the chariot races in *Roman Scandal* were better than those in *Quo Vadis*.

Ella was on the committee of the Newlyn Art Gallery, where she exhibited in the summer and winter shows. The chairman was Charles Le Grice of Trereife (pronounced Treeve) and Stanhope Forbes was the 'Promoter'. The other committee members were Lamorna Birch, Reginald Dick, Mrs Maud Stanhope Forbes, Geoffrey Garnier, Eleanor Hughes, Hilda Quick, Charles Simpson and Borlase Smart. They are all well-known names today, the least familiar being Reginald Dick, who had taught enamelling at

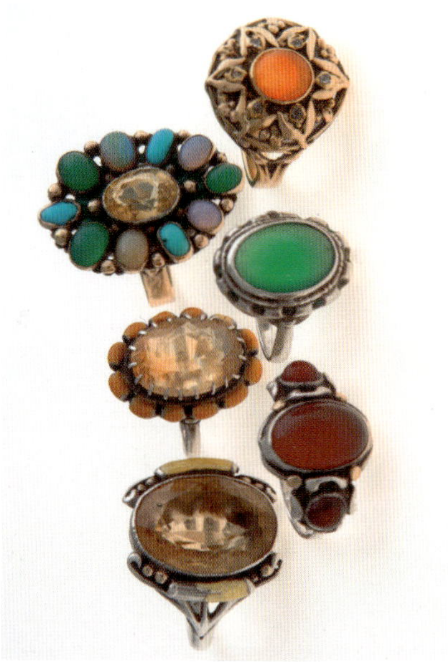

Silver and gold rings set with hardstones and semiprecious stones, one enhanced with enamel

the Newlyn Industrial class, and Hilda Quick, a Penzance artist who designed programmes and sets for the Minack theatre. In 1936 the committee decided to sacrifice the members' summer show and devote the whole of August to an ambitious exhibition of the Art Treasures of Cornwall. The names of the lenders read like a roll-call of the great families of the county: Bolitho, Borlase, Clifden, Falmouth, Le Grice, Molesworth, Paynter, Pendarves, St Levan, Tyringham, Vyvyan, Williams. Scattered amongst them are some of the artistic community: Miss Cade, Geoffrey Garnier, Mrs Norman Garstin, Mrs Gotch and her daughter Phyllis, now the Marquise de Verdières, Mrs Lee-Hankey, Emily Westrup, Quiller-Couch and Alfred Sidgwick.

Mrs Naper lent two embroidered bags of 1630, an Elizabethan chain bag and an etui, a prayer book of the time of Charles I and several pieces of silver, a George I bell, a George II coffee pot and a George III teapot. Mrs Garstin and Mrs Gotch were widows; Mrs Naper was not, and yet the loans from Charles and Ella were attributed only to her even though they had come from Charlie's family. Charlie never joined in, keeping himself at a distance from the rest of society.

However, he went to the opening of the exhibition, concentrating on the exhibits and keeping people at bay by pencilling notes in his catalogue. Against Sir Courtenay Vyvyan's Canaletto of Venice he wrote 'Not so', and against his *View of Trelowarren* by an unknown artist he scribbled 'awful'. The John Opie self-portrait belonging to the Penzance publisher and bookseller J.A.D. Bridger was a 'v bad copy'. A portrait by Zoffany, who had painted Charlie's forebears, was 'pleasant, awful frame', while Miss Cade's Hondekoeter still life was 'horrible and not by above'. An early seventeenth-century conversation piece by Jacob Duck was 'very nice, obviously by someone else'. Less than halfway through the exhibition he gave up.

From the notes in the catalogue Charlie appears extremely knowledgeable about art, someone who knows a Duck from a Hondekoeter. However, one wonders whether he was always correct and this document reveals a rather strange and sardonic turn of mind in its certainty of being right and its extreme dismissiveness of the exhibition.

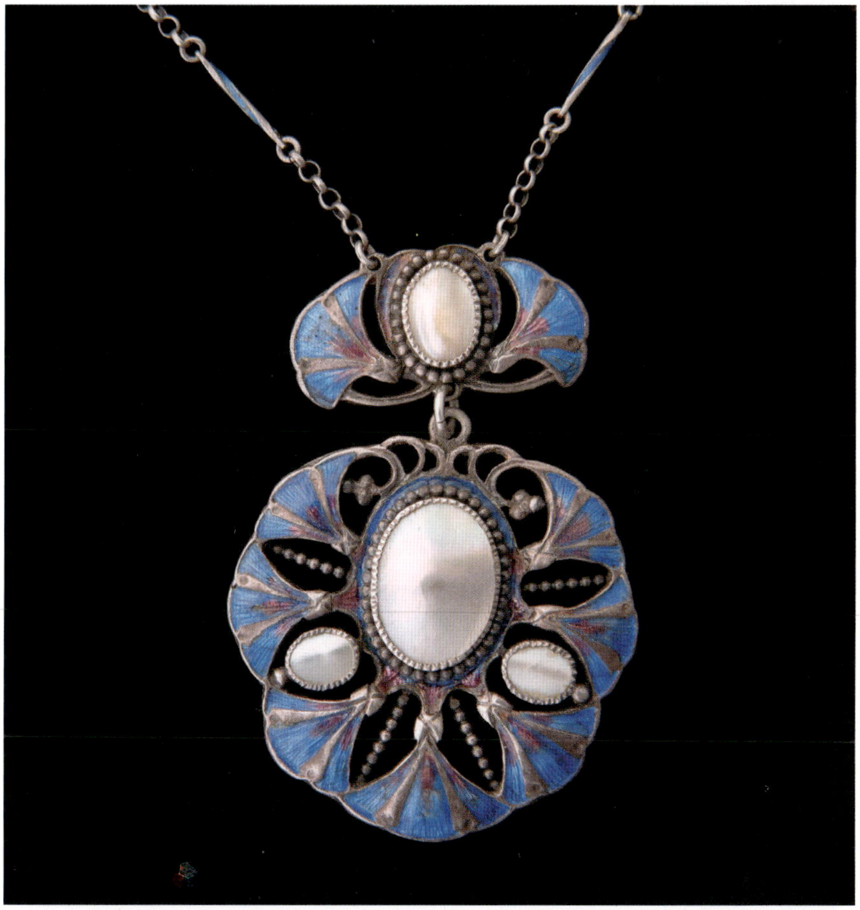

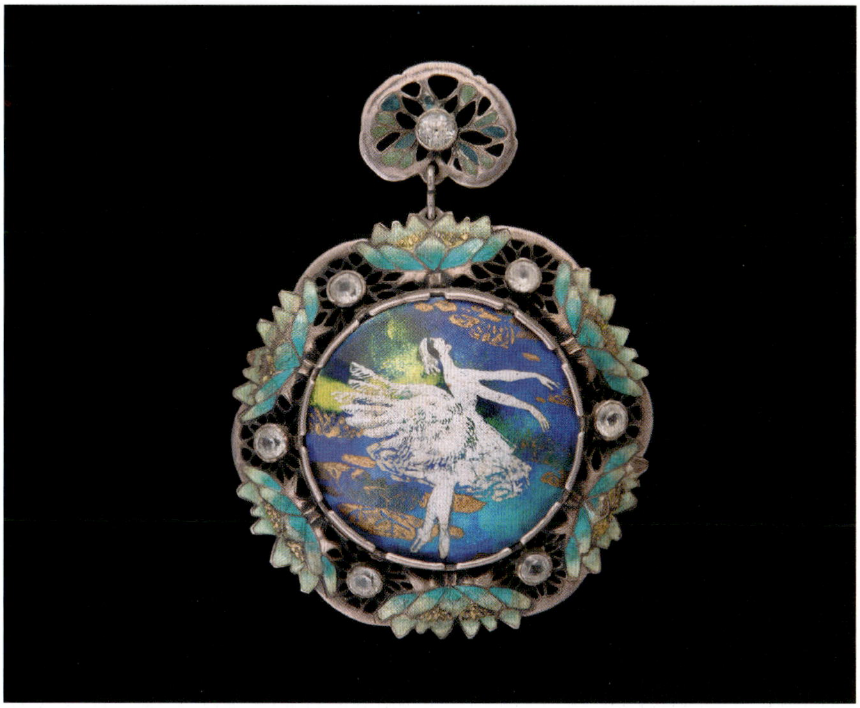

TOP
A silver pendant enamelled in lilac and blue, set with mother of pearl

An enamelled plaque designed by Laura Knight, set within an enamelled waterlily mount, enhanced with applied gold and clear cut stones. Signed LK & EN 1915

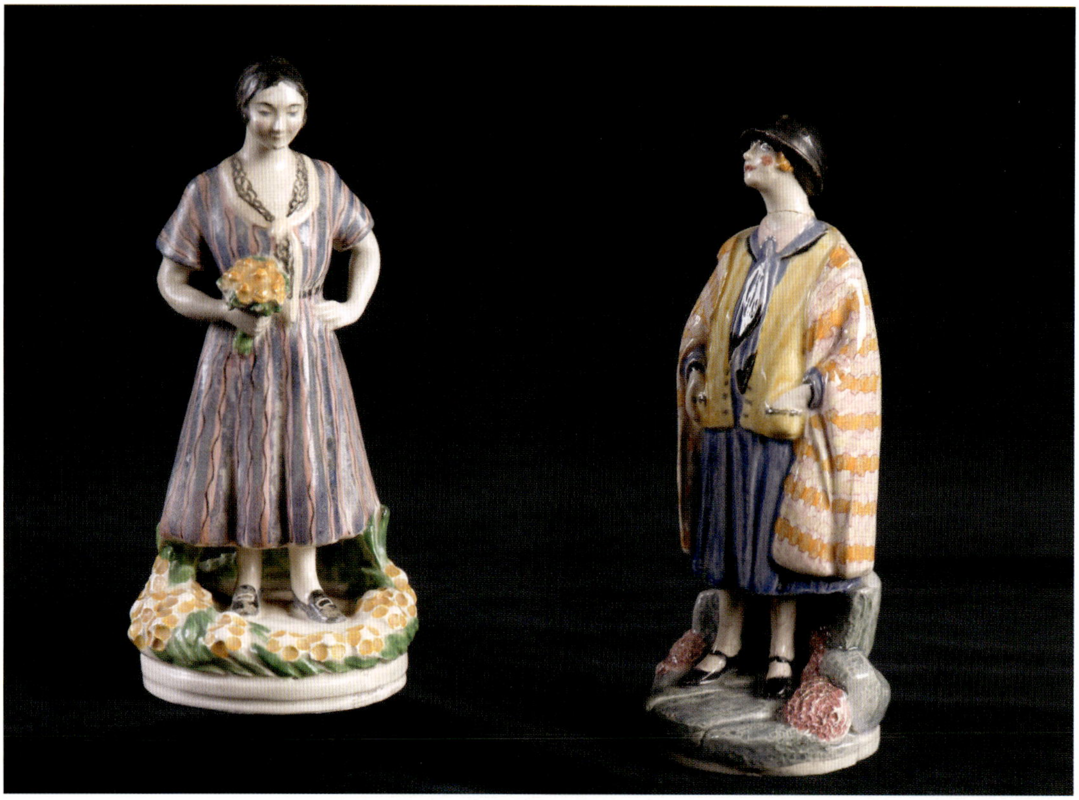

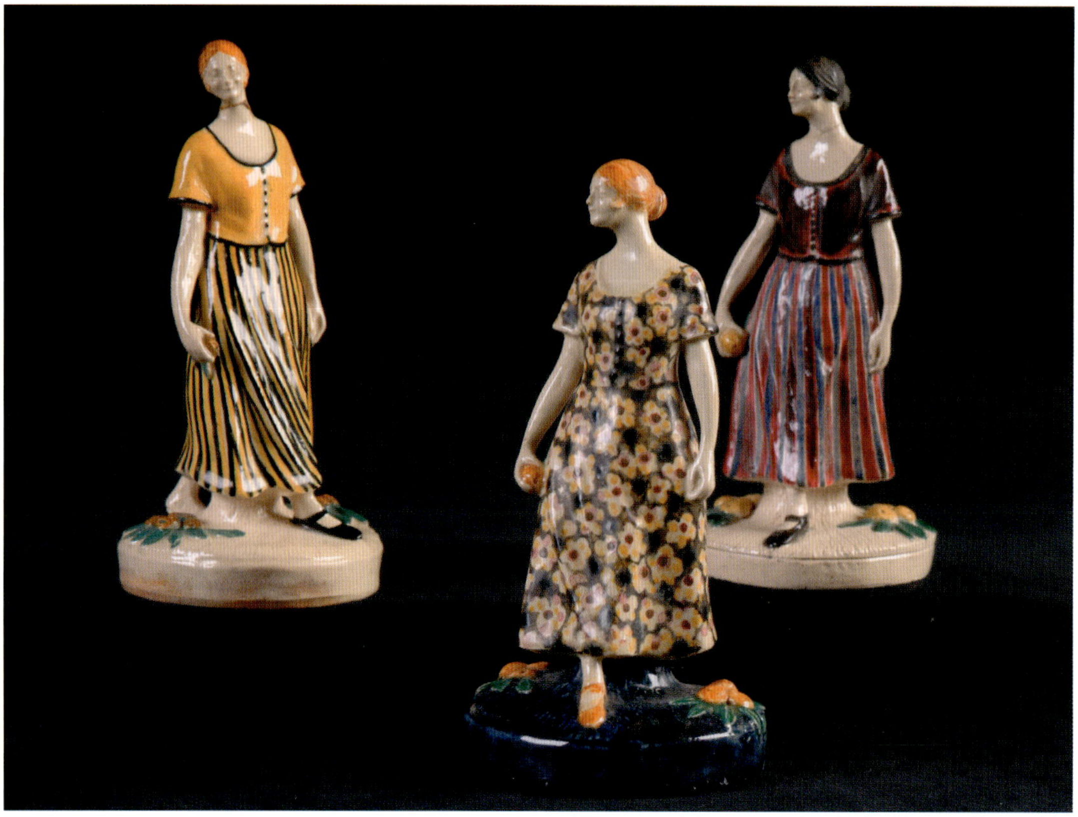

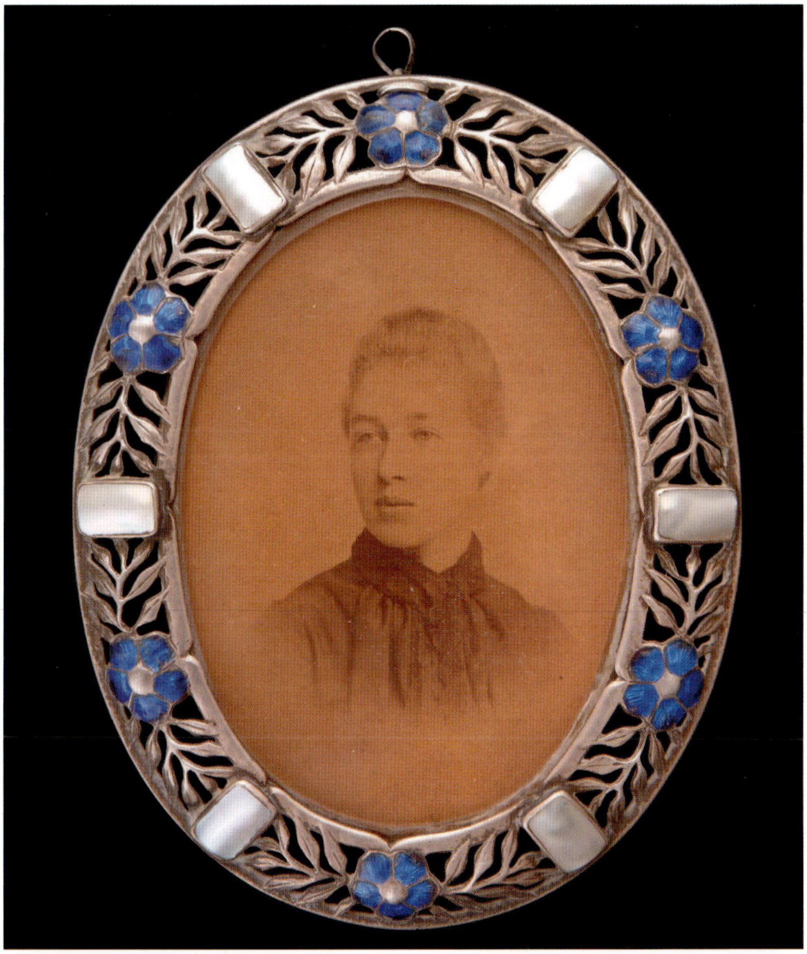

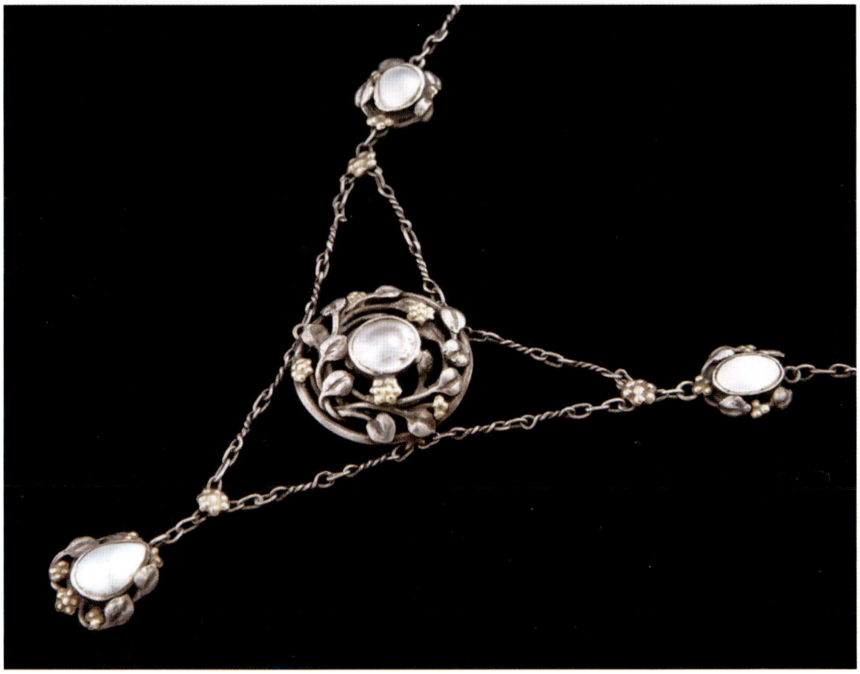

TOP
Oval silver photograph frame set with mother of pearl and with blue enamelled flower heads

A silver pendant set with mother of pearl and with applied gold flowerhead decoration

OPPOSITE
Ceramic figures made by Ella of herself and Laura Knight, 8 in

Further self portraits by Ella, $5^{1}/_{2}$ in

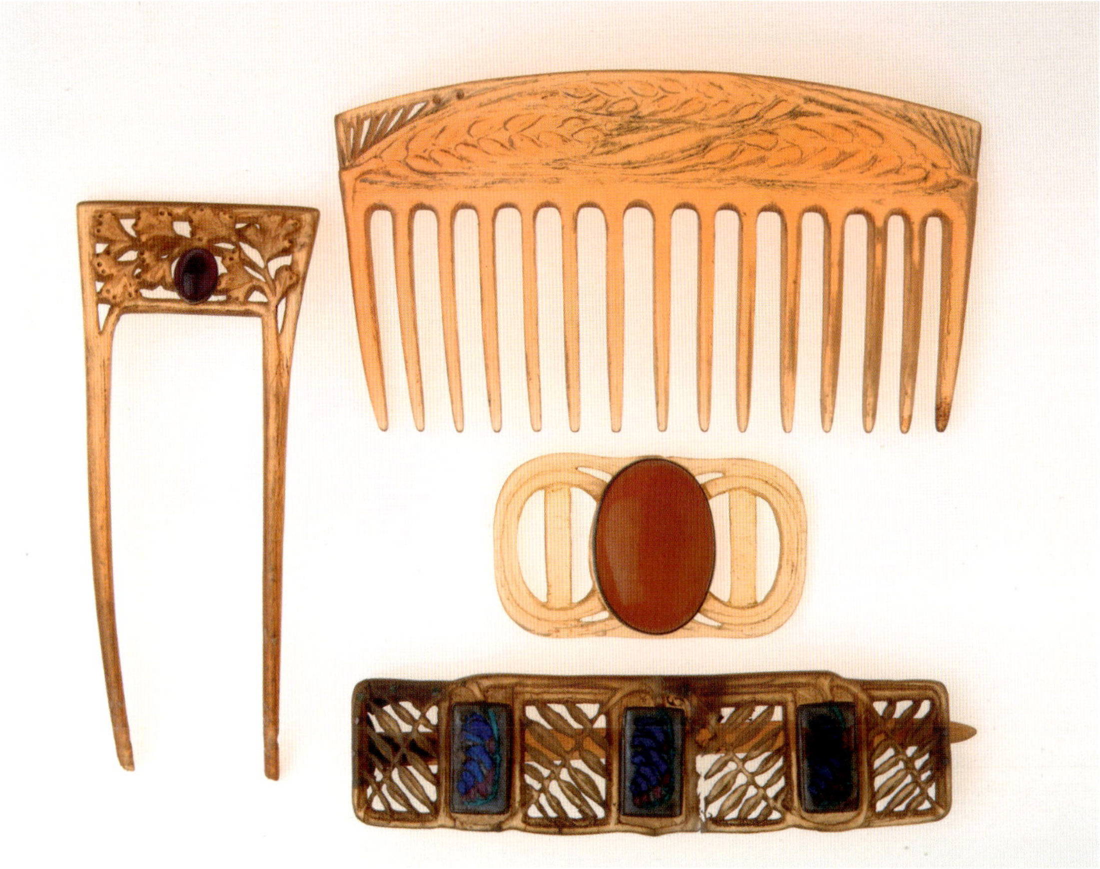

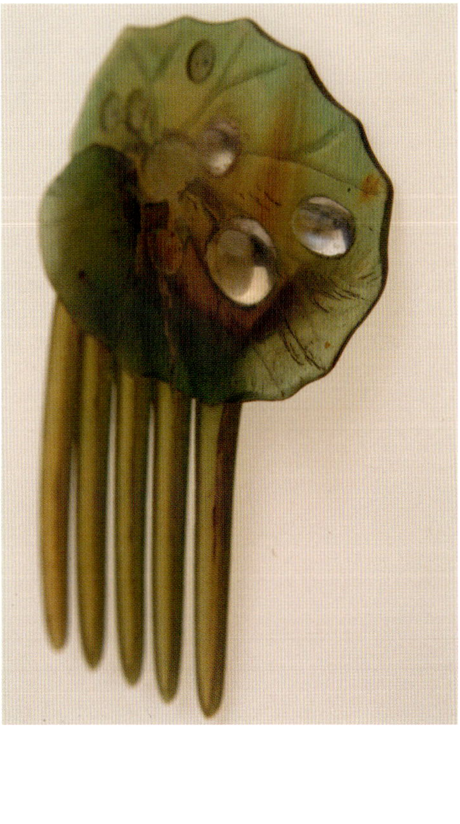

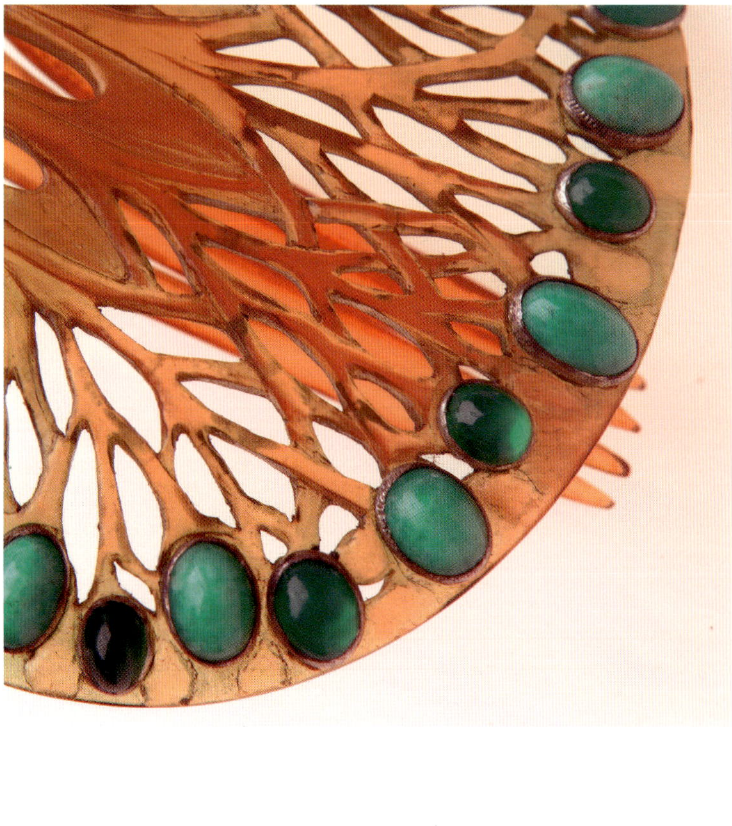

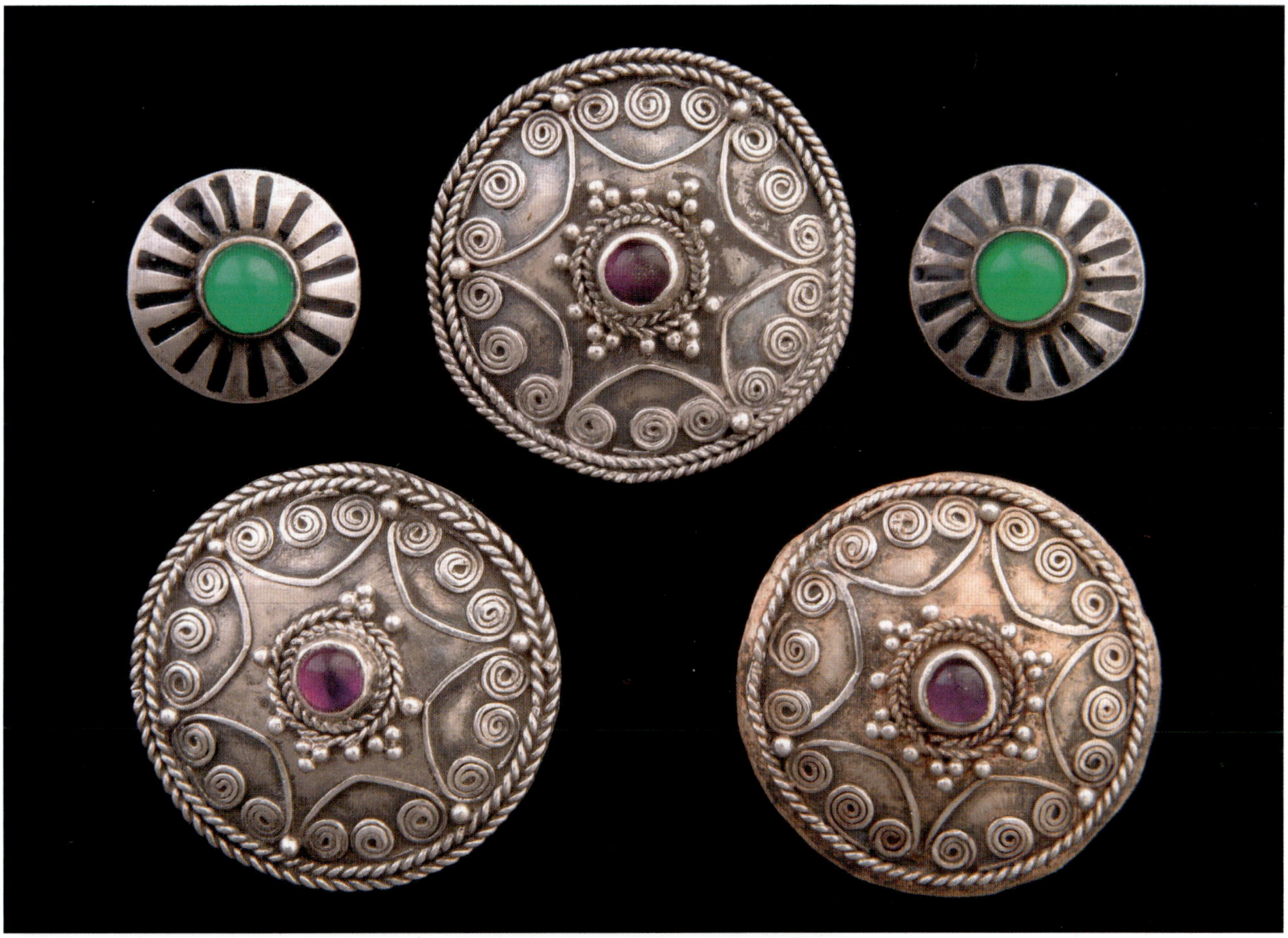

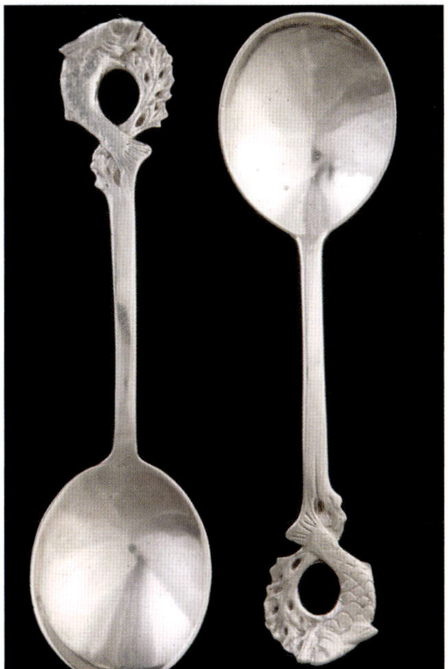

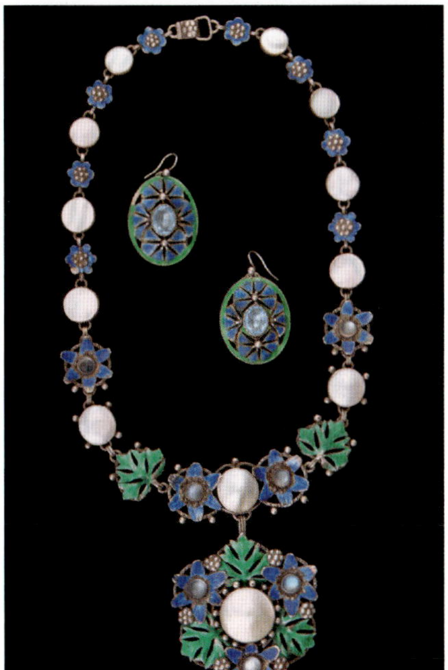

ABOVE
A pair of silver and black enamelled buttons set with green chalcedony; three silver buttons set with amethyst

LEFT
Spoons
Ella Naper

A blue and green silver necklace set with moonstones and mother of pearl, stamped on reverse; a pair of blue and green enamelled silver pendant earrings set with aquamarine

OPPOSITE
Three horn hair ornaments and horn scarf ornament set with amber

Two horn hair combs

Enamel work by Ella Naper
and Laura Knight 1915

OPPOSITE
Pots, jugs and bowls produced by the
Lamorna Pottery c.1925

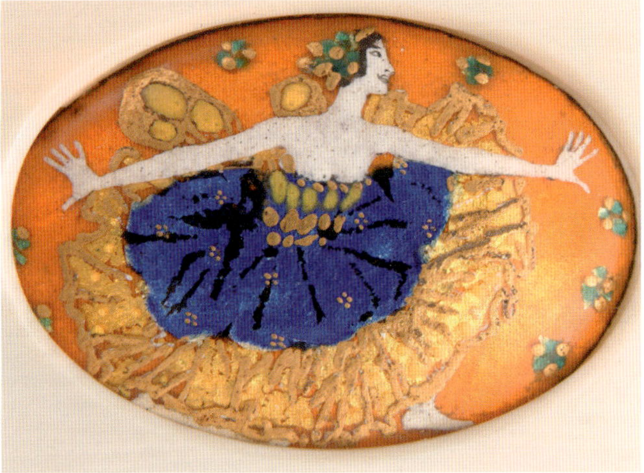

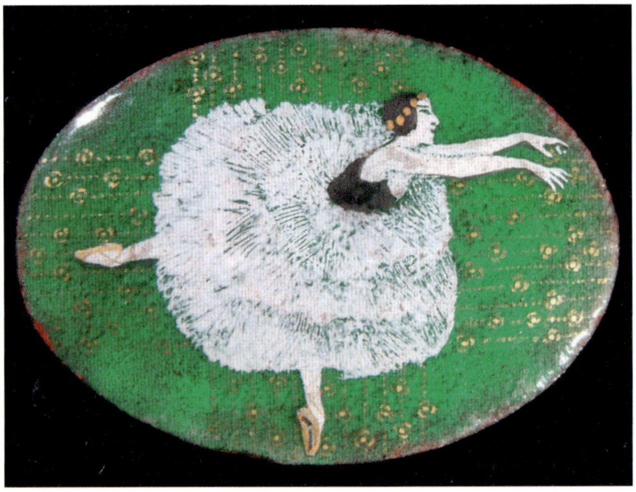

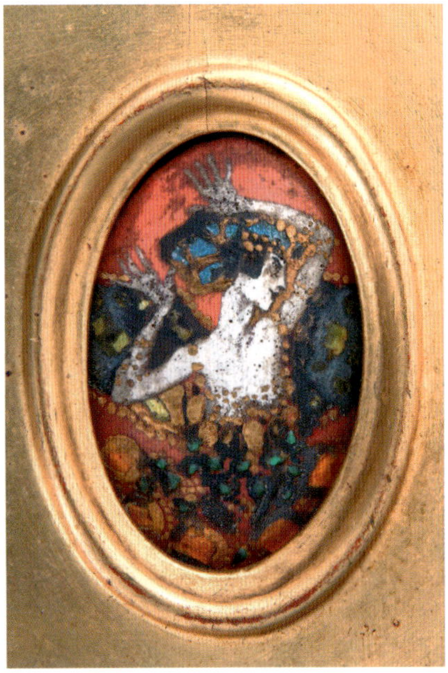

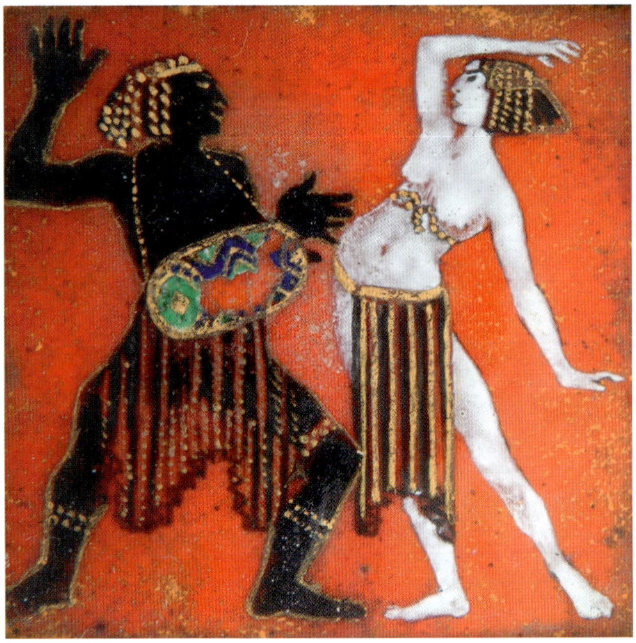

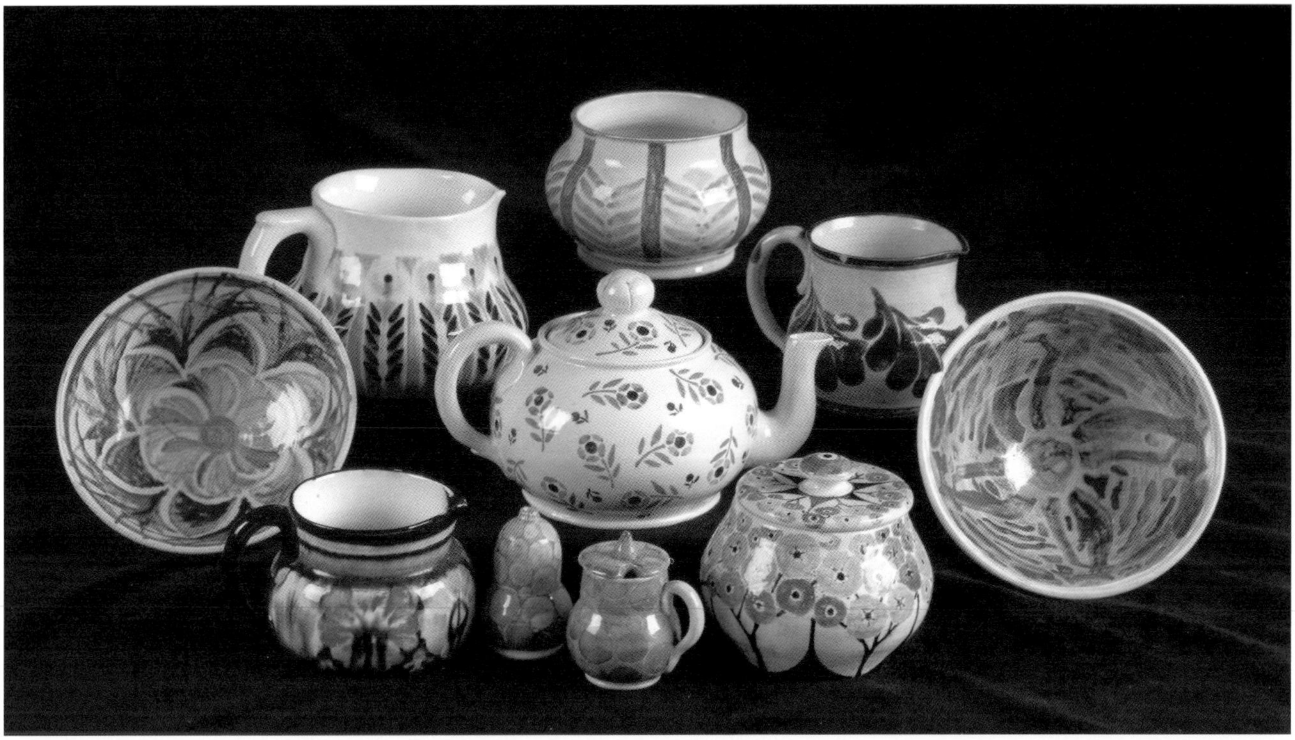

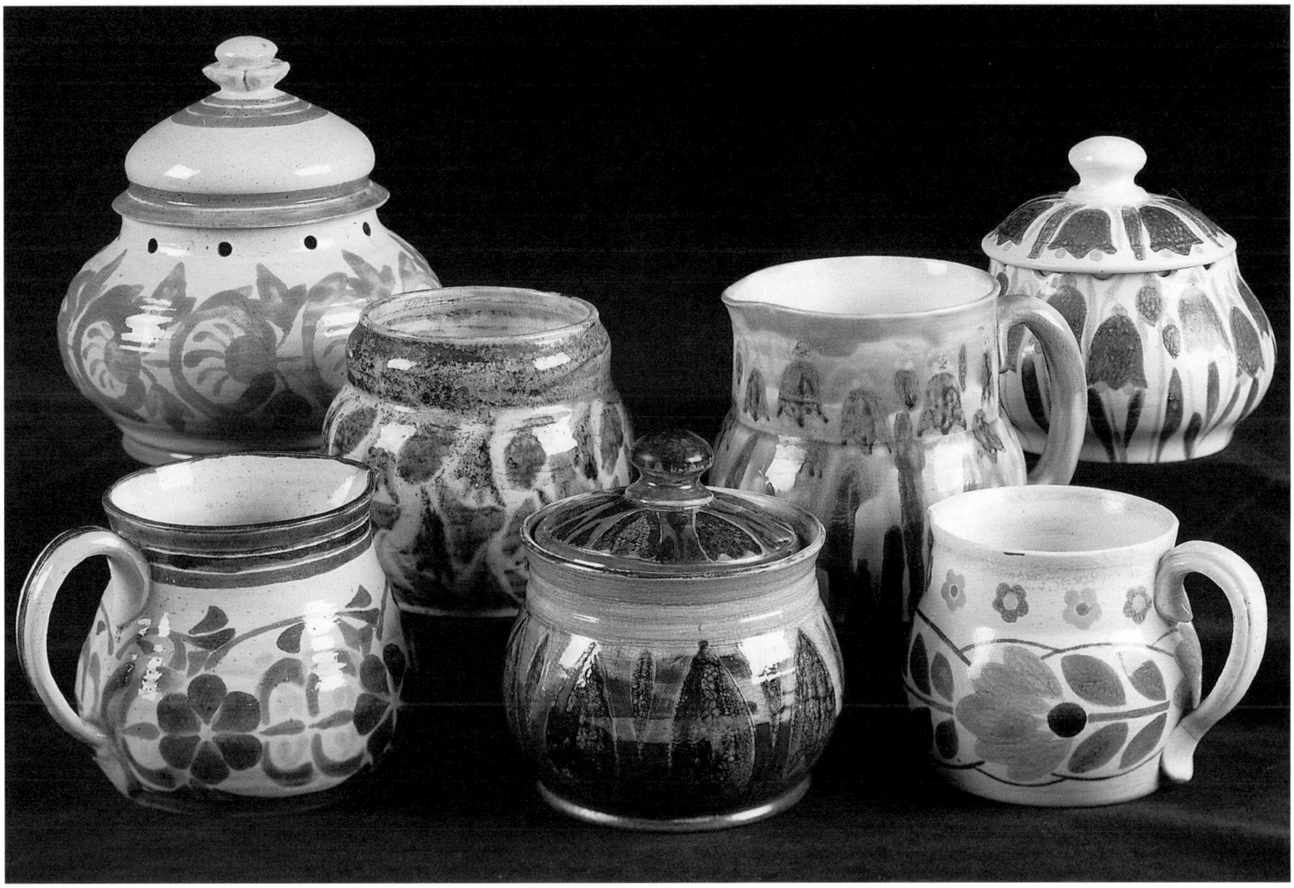

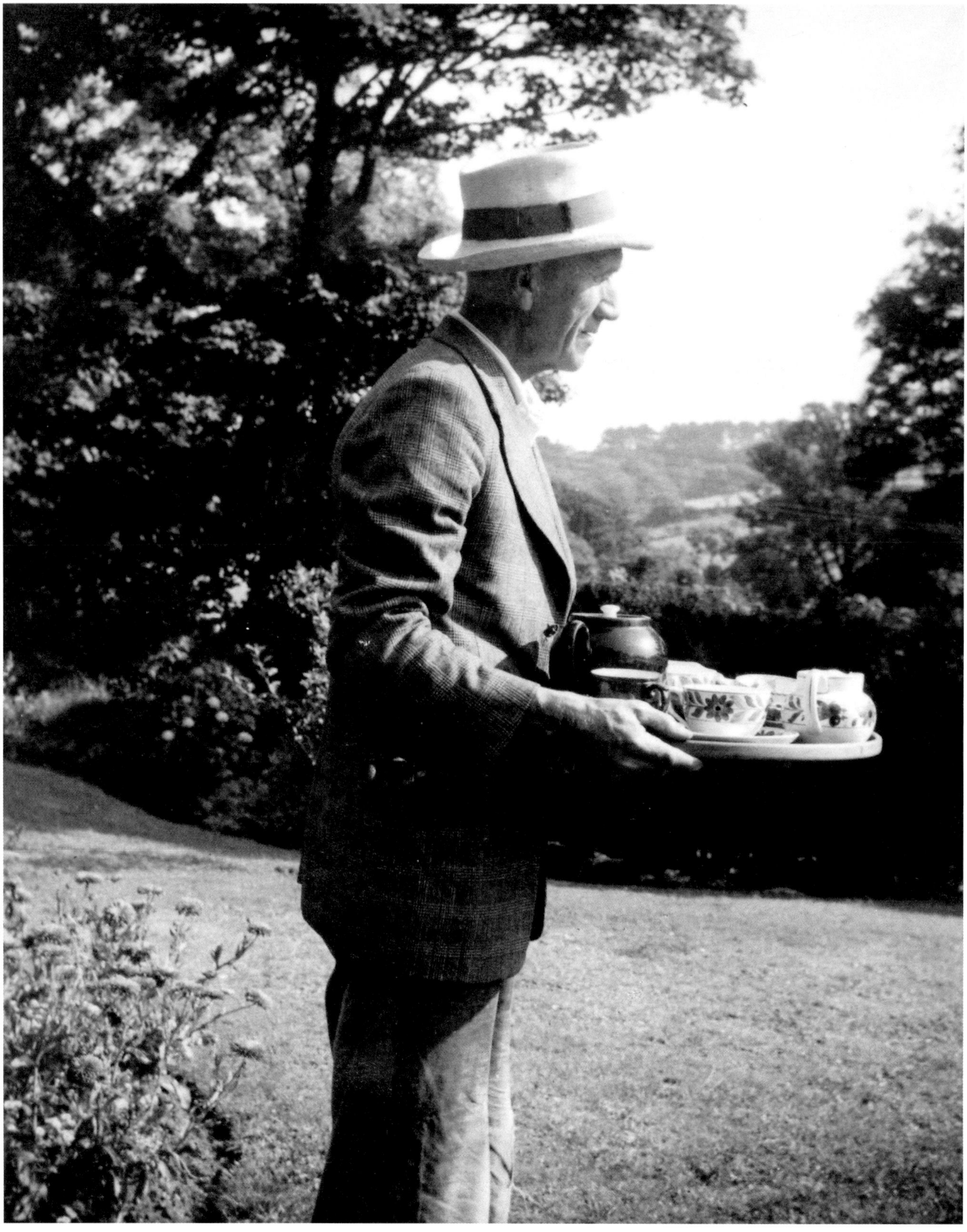

Apples and Honey: The Second World War

CHAPTER ELEVEN

Ella had made a mayoral chain for the Mayoress of Penzance in 1933 and enamelled prefects' badges for Penzance Girls' Grammar School. But the Newlyn Art Gallery was now the main outlet for her jewellery. In the summer exhibition of 1938 she entered twenty-one pieces of which sixteen sold for a total of £30.10.6. The last entry in her account book is for July 1939 when she sold five rings, a pair of earrings and two scarf pins for £6.15.6. Two months later war was declared with Germany and Ella never exhibited again, making new pieces only for family and friends or by special request.

Once the war began she and Charlie put their main effort into growing food. They listened to the talks of Mr Middleton, the Radio Gardener, and cut out his articles in the *Listener*, pasting them into the pages of her old ledger. Ella made a new label to stick on the cover, and ACCOUNTS became GARDEN. The articles were about growing marrows in the air-raid shelter, the enemies in the garden, apples for amateurs. Charlie had taken up apple culture some years before when disheartened by his catch at fishing, and during the war he planted more trees.

In May 1940 Mr Middleton wrote an article recalling nostalgically the old country villages of his childhood, where the orchards and gardens were humming and buzzing with bees and 'our old lime tree in June sounded like the deep diapason note of a great organ'. 'Wherever there is a garden there ought to be a beehive,' he wrote and perhaps this was what inspired Charlie to keep bees. He joined – Charlie who never joined anything, but wartime circumstances were exceptional – the West Cornwall Beekeepers' Association, went to meetings and talks and kept five hives. 'No 1 swarmed – hived in no 4,' their diary records in May. 'No 3 working on 7 combs, no 4 working on 5 ½ combs.' On 30 July he collected fifteen pounds fourteen ounces of honey from one hive. In October he is putting sugar in the hives, in November candy, a jam jar over the feed hole. 'Feed till fruit trees in blossom.' Nell's

OPPOSITE
Charlie in the garden at Trewoofe

daughter Maryella recalls the smell of apples and honey that came from the storeroom and filled the house.

They turned over more of the garden to vegetable crops in the 'Dig for Victory' campaign to make the country more self-sufficient in the production of food, though the far fields were still let to two women who had a nursery. They were known simply as Dodd and Palmer; they grew violets and anemones. Charlie and Ella dug the lower garden between the leat and the drive to Trewoofe Manor, the part they called the 'garage garden' which had never been cultivated before. The diary entries for one month give an impression of how busy they were:

March

1	Planted 140 garlic
2	Planted 230 garlic C finished Strawberry Bank
3	Planted 160 Strawberry runners on big bank
5	Planted 116 Strawberries
8	Sowed Brussel Sprouts, Leeks, Purple Sprouting, Broccoli, Lettuce, Pioneer Peas
9	Sowed Carrot and Turnips, 1/2 row each
12	Dug big bed
16	Bone meal to Rhubarb
18	Planted 100 onions
19	Planted 99 onions, Turnips and Lettuce showing, also P.S. Brocolli, Broad beans thro. Netted B. Sprouts and P.S.B.
20	Planted 60 onions
21	Sowed Cuthberts White Spanish Onions and Woolworths White Spanish
30	Started clearing Pond

Although they worked hard, they could still appreciate the setting of their garden looking down through the trees to the old slate roofs of the manor and farm house. 'PERFECT SPRING DAY' records Ella on Saturday 15 March 1941, 'Daffs at their best,' a week later. The war gave added poignancy to the beauty of their home.

A bomber was brought down into the sea off Porthcurno and when the daffodils were still in full bloom a German plane dropped a bomb on The Minack House, prominent on the cliff top. No one in the Cade household was hurt. In Berkshire during a night raid on London a plane unloaded its bombs over Ascot, some falling on the roof of Swinley Edge and in the garden. The very next day Maryella left with her nanny for Trewoofe, but Aunt Ella had two evacuees from Plymouth who slept in the second bedroom. After dark the refugees from Ascot walked along Kale Alley under the tall trees to Trewoofe Orchard, where Maryella said goodnight to a very old man (Alfred Sidgwick) and went to bed by the light of an oil lamp. The two boy evacuees went home after six weeks, but Maryella had already returned to Berkshire. For a while Ruth Simpson's daughter Leonora worked as a Land Girl at Boskenna, looking after a small herd of dairy cattle. Not liking the accommodation on the farm she stayed at Trewoofe over the weekends.

Ella went to a meeting at St Buryan to organise rest centres, in the next days canvassing the village for helpers. She joined a work party making clothes for those whose homes had been bombed and who had lost everything. Her industrious needle was as busy as ever. She made dressing gowns for herself and Charlie out of old blankets, and a little later one for Maryella. They were embroidered in brightly-coloured wools with random designs of butterflies and flowers.

If one developed a hole, a cigarette burn perhaps in Charlie's, she went around it with a buttonhole stitch, added petals and turned it into another colourful flower. They were not just examples of the wartime maxim, 'Make do and Mend'; they were works of art in their own right. She made dolls for Nell to sell at fund-raising bazaars in Ascot. They were about eighteen inches tall, made from old lisle stockings and the odd scraps of material that she always collected. The dresses – complete with underclothes – were beautifully made. She kept one for herself, or perhaps it did not sell and was sent back to Trewoofe.

Charlie helped out on the farm throughout the war, spending days planting potatoes and later lifting them, haymaking and harvesting in addition to the work in his own garden. They recorded their crops in the back of the 1942 diary: some fifty-five pounds of broad beans, nine pounds of French beans, thirty pounds of peas, eight pounds of tomatoes and sixty-three pounds of strawberries. The garlic they supplied to Harrods.

Because of the war, Lamorna in some ways was very quiet. With few visitors and little traffic because of petrol rationing it reminded them of how it was when they first arrived thirty years earlier. Ella had tea with the Birches and the Harveys, the Simpsons came for sherry.

In the middle of the war Ella 'went to Gert, got picture of Harold's.' It was a view looking down on to Newlyn harbour from the fields high above. Harold had died in 1941 and Gert must have given it to Ella as a memorial. Belle Leader stayed for a week. Dod Procter brought over her lunch, Ella had tea with Golly in Mousehole, where Golly and Dorothy were less busy at their bird hospital. Most of the patients were oiled seabirds and now ships were not releasing oil at sea because the slick could reveal their presence to enemy submarines.

It was all far less eventful than Laura Knight's wartime years.
The War Artists' Advisory Committee, chaired by Sir Kenneth Clark, offered Laura more work than she could undertake: a poster for the Women's Land Army, a portrait of a WAAF officer who had been decorated, followed by others. For the Air Ministry she painted the girls at work repairing a barrage balloon 'like a great silver toad'; for the Ministry of Munitions *Ruby Loftus Screwing a Breach Ring in a Bofors Gun*. She was commissioned to paint a bomber crew taking off in a Stirling. The paintings are now in the Imperial War Museum.

She and Harold were living at the Park Hotel, Colwall, a few miles from Malvern, from where Laura writes in the winter of 1944.
'I wish I could see the primroses [in Cornwall]. I can imagine them pushing up in the cracks between the granite steps. I wish I could see the newly planted orchard and trees and the bees. I hope you get enough to eat…
It must be hard away in Lamorna where you cannot get any extra meals at any kind of restaurant… I wonder how are all our friends, the Hughes, John and Mornie, Dod, Gert. I wonder if you have time to make your beautiful jewellery or if you can get materials. I wonder if Charlie's bees and gardening leave him lots of time for painting.'

'We went to London 2 weeks ago for a spell, but only stayed two days…
We were only 2 minutes walk away from a rocket bomb on the first night at 11.10. Only the top windows and one other in our hotel went – we were lucky – 2 steel and concrete buildings saved us from the blast. In other directions the blast went ½ mile. The next night we heard another further off. London is dire – Are your relations still there? I hope not. Of course these rocket bombs do not do the colossal damage of an airplane raid, but I would rather be in a raid in a shelter than never know where and when these deadly things are going to drop without warning…'

In Lamorna, the greatest threat was now from the American army, massing along the south coast in preparation for the invasion of France. The army chose the cove as a suitable place to practise landings and were planning to blow up the harbour wall, but then it was called off and Lamorna settled back into its usual leafy, water-loud calm. On Victory in Europe Day, 9 May 1945, Charlie and Ella planted out French beans and cut the grass.

Aunt Wiggy

CHAPTER TWELVE

On 1 November 1941 Ella went into Penzance: 'Dr to look at head,' she wrote in her diary. She makes no mention of any visits to surgeries or hospitals for another fifteen years, though she might occasionally be 'indoors with snivel' for a few days. In fact she had a swelling on the top of her head which grew into a lump. It was not painful and at first did not interfere with her life. She dismissed it as a 'carbuncle'.

After the war she had a big spring-clean, washing the ceilings, scraping the walls and distempering. She painted the bathroom and kitchen, then the front door, hall cupboard and small windows in her usual Lamorna blue. She whitewashed the larder and made new curtains for the bedrooms. On a single day she mended an old sofa, a ballcock and a cigarette lighter.

They continued to grow vegetables on a wartime scale, filling the back pages of notebooks and diaries with plans of the garden divided into beds, each plot for main crop potatoes, leeks and onions measured in feet, each row of peas, beans, turnips and carrots measured in inches. Charlie was always precise. The winter planning had then to be put into practice and recorded in the red *Sunday Times* 'My Garden Diary'. They were interested in books on self-sufficiency, in growing their own tobacco duty-free, in a formula for a herbal smoking mixture of coltsfoot leaves, clover flowers and rose petals. They used more wood instead of coal. When they had a delivery of coal the lorry had to drive across a field and through a gate in the stone hedge to reach the coalhouse. During the war a spring gale had blown down a large ash tree; it provided plenty of logs, though it meant all the work of sawing, splitting and wheelbarrowing. The produce of the garden had to be dealt with as well. The bees yielded 152 pounds of honey in 1947. Ella made plum and blackcurrant jam, redcurrant jelly and tomato chutney; she bottled fruit and made wine.

Day after day she wrote 'C on pond' and then eventually 'Pond full and lovely.' Like her friends Pog and Dorothy Yglesias, Ella loved birds and she noted peewits in the garden, long-tailed tits by the lower compost heap, goldfinches in the orchard. On 30 April she saw the first swallows and in July three thrushes hatched in the nest in the bay tree. One winter's day she persuaded a great tit to feed from her hand and from then on the robins and tits would tap on the windows to be fed.

In February 1947 she went to Ascot for the wedding of Nell's son Peter Male to Pat Payne and it snowed all week during that worst winter of the century. The newly-weds came to Trewoofe in March, and in May Charlie and Ella went back to Dozmary Pool. 'Lovely day,' wrote Ella; it must have been very moving to return to the place they had discovered during the first summer of their marriage, and where they had spent youthful carefree days with their friends.

Ella often returned to Ascot, either alone or with Charlie. In April 1956 they went together, driven up by the Scobeys. (Alfred Sidgwick had died in 1943 and Trewoofe Orchard after the war was occupied by Mary and Dennis Scobey.) They become good friends of the Napers and often played bridge together in the evenings.

Ella had not told anyone else in Lamorna the reason for the visit. From Ascot she was going to St Bartholomew's Hospital, so close to where she and Charlie were married and where her niece now worked as an outpatients' clerk. Maryella had realised from the patients she saw and whose notes she read that a 'carbuncle' could be a melanoma and she persuaded her aunt to see a specialist. 'To Barts for advice,' Ella entered in the diary. The tumour on her head proved malignant and she went into the hospital the following day, to be operated on the next. 'Op', she wrote simply.

Charles waited anxiously at Swinley Edge. He busied himself in the large garden, cutting back the heather and getting rid of it on bonfires, a task he performed on every visit to Ascot as he believed no one else could do it properly. He writes reassuringly to Ella in hospital that he has been having a lovely time cutting and burning in the garden. Nell too tries to reassure her. She tells Ella that the two men, Jack and Charlie, 'get on so well together and are not the least trouble.'

News of Ella's serious operation had reached Lamorna. John and Maud Trewern lived at Trewoofe Farm and Mrs Trewern writes to Nell Male: 'We were all very sorry to hear about dear Mrs Naper. We never knew there was anything wrong with her. She was here with me two days before she went away and not a word poor dear how long have she known it.' Like everyone else she thinks of Charlie. 'How is Mr Naper I suppose he is thinking about home.' At the same time she writes to Ella: 'I'll bet Mr Naper is missing

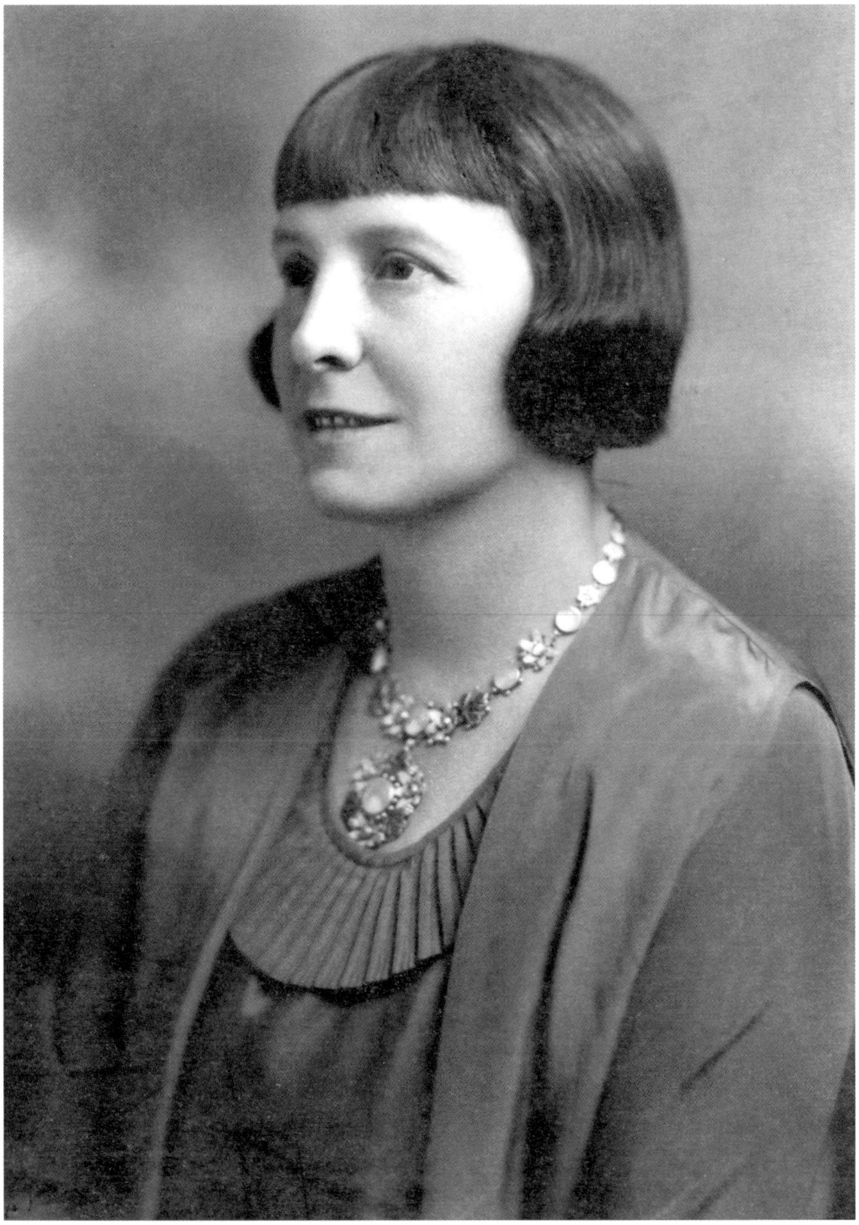

Ella's sister Nell wearing an example of Ella's jewellery

you. I know well what the men are like without the women. So hurry dear and get well.'

Three days after the operation Charlie and Nell went to St Bartholomew's and saw Ella; her head was shaven and bandaged and a skin graft had been taken from her thigh. No one expected Charlie to go to the hospital, but he visited every three days. Ella began to have visits from others, Alex, Edie and brother Harry and it was Alex and Maryella who brought her back to Ascot after two and a half weeks. A week later she began to go out, to Wisley and Virginia Water. She returned to St

Bartholomew's five weeks after the operation. All was well and they went back to Cornwall on the last day of May. It was a long time for Charlie to be away from Trewoofe.

Ella made a good recovery. She had to wear a wig until her hair grew again, and she signed her letters 'Aunt Wiggy'. When the following year Maryella married Francis Pigott, a doctor at St Bartholomew's, she transformed a pair of Georgian cuff-links into earrings, a ring and a brooch as a wedding present. It was also the year of Nell's tour to South Africa with the English bowls team. Ella made their enamelled badges, incorporating the English rose and the South African protea. But there was disturbing news from Lenox, Charlie's elder brother: their brother Edmond who lived near Chichester in Sussex was not well.

Edmond was suffering from anxiety or depression and was given electric shock treatment at Graylingwell Hospital. Then his illness was diagnosed as 'senile decay'. In January 1958 Lenox wrote from the Ship Hotel, Chichester, to say that Edmond had died.

Although he had heart trouble, arthritis and rheumatism – 'We are not getting any younger,' he reminds Ella – he busied himself settling Edmond's affairs, as he had not made a will. The estate was shared between himself and Charles; he put the house, Gorse Bank, Storrington, on the market and rather than sell the stocks and shares he thought it best to divide them into two roughly equal lists, A and B, and asked Charles to choose one or the other. Charlie would not do anything about it. Lenox had to write to Ella to get a response. Edmond had been looked after for years by his servant Alice, who had been paid only two pounds a week. Lenox thought she ought to be rewarded out of the money from the sale of the house. He wrote to Ella once more: 'Would you kindly let Charles see this and if he has anything to say he must write it himself. I don't see why you should be bothered with our letters!' But Charlie wanted to shut Edmond's death out of his mind. He had begun travelling the same road himself.

Charlie

CHAPTER THIRTEEN

After Edmond's death Lenox continued to write to Ella rather than to Charlie, putting in a banknote at Christmas for her 'to get something you want'. Some years earlier he had sent a card which showed their house at Malmesbury in Wiltshire, 'so that you can see our little home,' wrote Daphne, regretting that they never came to visit. The 'little home' looked quite a grand Cotswold manor. But now it had become too much for them, and it was impossible to get 'a useful, all-round creature to help cook and run the kitchen'. They moved to a bungalow nearer their daughter Meriel in Gloucestershire. Lenox had inherited Loughcrew, the now rather depleted estate in Ireland, when his cousin William died without issue, but made it over to his son Nigel.

A year after Edmond's death Lenox wrote from his bed, where he was resting his heart, a chatty letter about the family. Loughcrew had been burned down again. The last fire he thought was in 1888, when Willy their cousin was a small boy. He very gallantly dashed in and rescued a pair of new gloves. Lenox had seen a report in *The Times* of the sale of their grandfather's hunting pictures by John Ferneley. The large one fetched £1,800 at Christie's, the smaller one of hunt servants made £1,000, both bought by Ackermann's. Their grandfather, as far as he recalled, paid £60 and £40 for them. The money would be sent to relatives in Australia. He was going to have Edmond's name added to the family tombstone.

All the effort of keeping the family together and informed came from Lenox. Charles showed no interest in his relatives, never went to weddings nor funerals, never wrote letters. Charlie was a difficult man to know. He was so uncommunicative that probably no one but Ella really understood him. Those who remember the pair knew them only in old age, and they always comment on his utter dependence upon Ella. But when they were younger she often went away independently, spending three weeks with her family in Bromley or Ascot, a week with Dofferty Cade at The Minack, leaving Charlie to look after himself.

In the nineteen twenties when Ella was in London he writes to say that he is enjoying his evenings with Laura and Golly. He has seen Emily who said Mrs Sidgy was coming up to ask him to supper. 'I am to ask the Hughes for Thursday from Laura – This letter seems full of suppers. Love darling, C.' This does not sound like someone with no friends and unable to cope by himself. What happened to Charlie that he became so dependent on Ella and so completely cut off from family and friends?

Many of his generation were deeply affected by the war, the experience remaining with them to the end of their lives. The Napers' neighbour Frank Heath was a changed man when he returned to Menwinnion. Ever afterwards he lacked energy and will-power and was often moody and uncommunicative, though he continued to paint sunny and colourful pictures. But Charlie had been lucky. The war for him had been more like an eighteenth-century gentleman's Grand Tour. He saw little or no action, none of the horrors of trench warfare. His insecurity must have had deeper roots.

Not much is known of his childhood. Charlie had the upbringing of children of the privileged classes in late Victorian England. It was normal for such children to have little contact with their parents, who remained remote and distant figures. Their experience of affection was often from a nanny, from whom they were separated when they were sent away to boarding school. Such an education produced the leaders of the Empire, strong unemotional men who made good soldiers and administrators of the colonies. But there was a high casualty rate. For a sensitive child with artistic leanings it was just as traumatic as a battlefield.

As a young man Charlie spent seven years as a student, first of architecture and then of painting. In the year of his marriage he had a painting accepted by the Royal Academy. Ella was presumably the model for *The Lace-Maker*; it was priced at twenty-five pounds and did not sell. It is surprising that he did not follow this with other entries in the pre-war years. They were living at Great Tree, Looe; Ella was producing her jewellery, he had nothing else to do but paint and fish. The war intervened and after his return he took his time before exhibiting again, showing *Pordenick, Land's End* in 1929. It was not for sale. He entered one painting a year for the next three years, *Near Land's End* priced at two hundred pounds, *Treen Sands, near Land's End* which was not for sale and *Near Porth-Curno, Land's End* which was also not for sale. And then he entered a painting which was rejected.

Lamorna Birch wrote from the Knight's house in St John's Wood, his only letter addressed to Charlie, to say how sorry he was that his picture wasn't hung. 'I can't understand it… I told several members of the hanging committee what pigs they were – Talmage especially, and he said he hadn't seen it … It makes me wonder what they do see when I see the muck they've hung. I'm very sorry indeed old man.'

Selection at the RA was notoriously haphazard, with porters trundling pictures past the committee members at a fast rate. Through living at Lamorna, Charles knew some important painters but he never cultivated the influential figures who could make sure that he was not overlooked. To be rejected once was no sign of failure; it was not a disaster. But Charlie never submitted anything to the Royal Academy again.

This minor reverse did not spur him on to greater efforts. Instead of fighting back he retreated into his shell. 'We were sorry not to see any of Charlie's paintings,' wrote Laura Knight, striking an ominous note in a thank-you letter after staying at Trewoofe. Charlie had found some pretext to keep them out of the studio. He became obsessively secret about his work. No one was allowed to see it.

Apart from Huddersfield in 1935, he didn't exhibit anywhere else, not even at the Newlyn Art Gallery where Ella was a committee member. It is usually said that he was discouraged by adverse criticism. The only criticism was that implied by the Royal Academy rejection and, as Lamorna Birch assured him, that was no reflection on the quality of his work. Lamorna Birch, Harold and Laura Knight all thought that he was a good painter. His early drawing of Ella is as good as Harold's, his painting of Ella perched on a stool and playing the mouth-organ in the hut at Dozmary captures her spirit more than Laura's *Self and Nude* of the same time. His wife was sought as a model by other artists, but Charlie did no more portraits of her. The pool in the garden was painted by Birch, not by Charles. His best subject matter was to hand and he chose only to paint detailed studies of rock formations on the Cornish cliffs.

An artist must paint what he wants to paint and cannot be criticised for not painting the pictures that others might have wished. Charlie's choice could have been interesting; it moved away from the over-obvious and pretty subjects of second-generation Newlyn painters and in the geometry of cliffs, the patterns and shapes of rocks, looks ahead to the abstract painters. But his paintings do not break new ground. In their careful precision they express part of his nature that became more pronounced as time passed.

It is not a good idea for an artist to settle too comfortably in one place. Laura and Harold Knight found fame and fortune by leaving Lamorna, John

Birch was identified with the valley but always spent months of each year away from the county. 'Being too long anywhere is apt to dry up inspiration,' W.H. Davies said to Laura Knight to justify his restless moving from place to place. Charlie's career was one long drying-up as he became more and more set in his ways. Mary Scobey remembers Charlie as the most meticulous man she ever knew. If he was choosing a new stone for the side of the 'splash' he would spend hours finding and positioning it. If the fire needed making up he would tell Ella which lumps of coal to choose and exactly where to place them.

He was a creature of habit. Every morning Ella cleared the ashes from the grate but only Charlie could set the fire. After breakfast they rolled their ration of cigarettes for the day. Charlie would get through his supply first, though 'they both smoked like chimneys', and would then beg Ella for a 'ciggy'. They always had to have macaroni cheese on a certain day, the same fruit cake every week. For Charlie everything had to be under control, or his childhood insecurity could overwhelm him. His routines were a form of self-defence. Mary used to laugh at him, but she wondered what would have happened if he had married someone less 'amenable' than Ella.

Although they rejected class distinction in their way of life, it was part of their attraction for each other. Charles had public school manners, he had charm and an air of distinction which appealed to Ella and satisfied her fantasies about her father's background. For Charles, Ella's working-class origins meant that she was prepared to nanny him in a way that a woman of his own class would not. He needed her to love, protect and look after him, and Ella responded to need; she gave him all the care that she would have given to a child if she had had one. In return he worshipped her, as insecure people often need to lose themselves in something greater, a religion or political belief or another person. Ella Champion's 'Ex Libris' was strangely prophetic, showing a pet creature gazing adoringly at the beautiful Eve. She fulfilled the destiny she foresaw for herself and found it satisfying. Mary Scobey says that she never saw any tension between them. Charlie absolutely adored Ella and she would have done anything for him.

She accepted him as he was. He cut a hole in the bedroom floor so that he could lower a basket on a rope to the kitchen below, where Ella would load whatever he required and he could haul it up without getting out of bed. If a visitor came into the house, he would slip out by the studio's back door and escape across the fields to Grambla Barn where he would stay until he thought it safe to return. Although he sought open spaces it was a sort of agoraphobia, quite literally a fear of the market place. He never wanted to expose himself or his wares to the public.

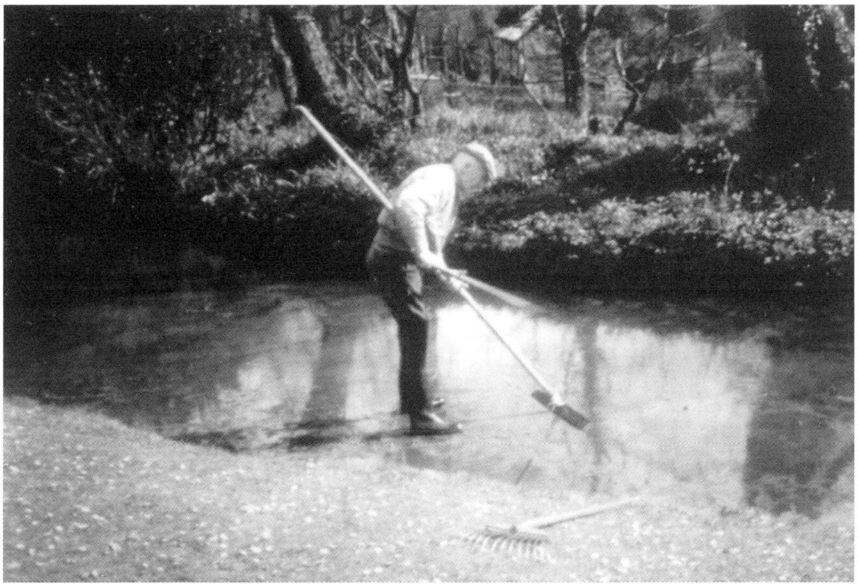

Charlie in old age

Towards the end of his life he went to the studio each day, dressed always in a fluffy woollen cardigan that Ella had knitted and corduroy trousers. The same painting remained on the easel for month after month and he sat in front of it, smoking a cigarette and staring at the canvas. In the garden he would stand in the pond 'for hours', a rake in his hand and a sun-hat on his head, as motionless as a heron. There he would stay until Bill Trewern came from the farm to lead him back to the house. Ella did not interfere. She did not fight his illness, not even when he burned his pictures.

The north light of the studio was leaking and in a storm they had to put buckets and basins beneath it to collect the rainwater. Ella arranged for the builders to come and repair it, and the day before they were due she told Charlie. Charlie panicked. They would see his paintings and he could not bear the thought of anyone seeing them. He took all the canvases that were stacked ten deep around the studio walls, the work of a lifetime, and piled them on the lawn. Then he set light to them.

The burning of paintings is a terrible thing: an act of utter despair, a sort of suicide. It also has a mythic dimension. The artist, whether composer, painter or writer, who destroys what he has created takes revenge upon a world which is not ready to accept his work or worthy of receiving it. But Charlie's bonfire was an act not so much of self-criticism or revenge as of dementia. Ella said that among the pictures he burned were a Munnings and a Laura Knight.

If Charlie's paintings had survived, would he have been 'discovered' after his death, an artist to rank with the best of Newlyn painters? We cannot know what was destroyed, only guess that some of the early work was comparable with Harvey or Forbes. *The Lace-Maker* of 1910 in subject matter could have been by either of them. Its loss is a great shame, and other works of this period went into the flames. But from the twenties Charlie seemed to concentrate entirely on cliff paintings and these would have been the larger part of the bonfire. A few survived, being in other parts of the house or simply overlooked, and they convey the sense of awe that the artist felt before the scale and antiquity of the cliffs. The best have tonal colour and atmosphere but others reveal too strongly his architectural training. His purpose is to record what is there: the light is flat, the proportions of the rocks are exact but the effect is as though they have been carefully put into place. The paint surface lacks life.

How could Ella let him burn his paintings? It was a question she was sometimes asked by those close to her. 'Charlie had created them,' she would reply. 'He had a right to do what he wanted with them.' For Ella, Charlie could always do what he wanted, but she did not allow for his confused state of mind.

He declined rapidly and was taken to Tehidy hospital near Camborne, where he died on 16 February 1968.

Ella

CHAPTER FOURTEEN

In the fifties Laura and Ella had drifted apart, rarely writing except for the exchange of Christmas cards. Laura was well-known after being chosen to record in drawings and paintings the Nuremburg War Trials and was always busy. They drew closer together again in old age and on 21 February 1968 Laura writes: 'I have just received Nell's letter telling of your dreadful loss…It is so hard to be left alone when half of your very self, in such a long partnership, is lost.' Ten days later she sent a card: 'Thought of you is in my heart all the time, that together with the great love I have for you and that possessed by everyone around you, may help you in some tiny way. I can see those primroses.'

Charlie's ashes were buried close to the pond. Laura sent another card: 'a word or two to tell you how constant is my thought of you and your bravery.' Ella had written to say how she had 'masses of work to do in both garden and house'. Laura said how much she wished she could be with her, but she had fallen and had to relearn how to walk with a stick.

Ella sent her boots for Christmas and Laura replies that they 'are a perfect fit and most classy to look upon'. She discusses the merits of various varnishes and says that she could teach Ella how to varnish properly.

In the year after Charlie's death Ella considered moving closer to her brother and sister at Ascot, possibly sharing a home with Nell. Alex and Edie took her away on holiday to Spain, where she bought a poncho. At home she acquired her last Pekinese and called her Fleur. 'It is a great joy to me to know that there is a possibility of your moving to London,' wrote Laura. But in the end she chose to stay on at Trewoofe in the house that she and Charlie had built and lived in for over fifty years, with the garden that they had created around it.

Soon after the first anniversary of Charlie's death Laura wrote again, as though she knew it would be one of her last letters and attempting some sort

Ella at Nell and Jack's golden wedding, 1969

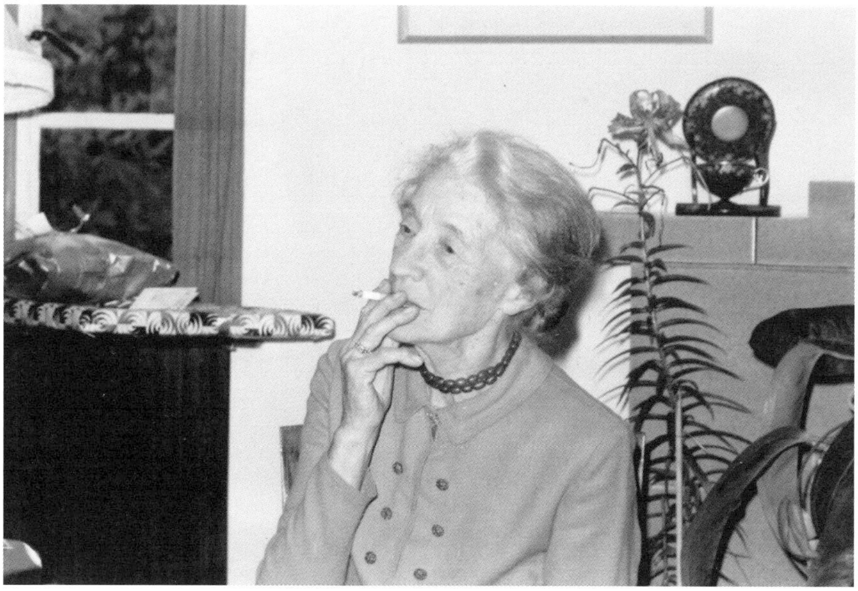

of summing-up. 'I know well the hardship it is to be the one left behind and you, like myself, would choose that it should be that way. I simply cannot tell you the vast delight your visits to me here in London gave to me. It is impossible to find words to express my joy in renewing the unbreakable tie that existed between us. Do you remember the old car that took us all four to the moors with a bed covering the running board, and how I piled into the heap after being chief witness of Bloat Munning's death, and I could do nothing but laugh and weep at the same time. God bless and keep you, dearest Ella.' She wishes that she could be more help to her, 'but unfortunately I am rather too much of an antiquity to be other than a possible responsibility'.

Laura refused though to recognise her 'antiquity' and was working on the preparations for an exhibition in June at The Upper Grosvenor Galleries, '75 Years of Painting'. She writes to tell Ella about it and hopes that she will come. Ella sends her a bunch of primroses. She writes again to ask if she can borrow for the exhibition the picture of a little boy that Charlie bought from her.

It is quite small, a fair-haired child standing in a rock pool, his body wet and gleaming, his clinging trunks like a loincloth. It has the name Bob on the back and is thought to be Algernon Newton's son Robert, who grew up to be the well-known actor. 'I believe it is one of my best works done at that period,' wrote Laura. 'I do hope you are not too lonely.' Ella sent the painting but could not have gone to the opening of the exhibition, because Laura sends a quick card: 'I am on television this evening at six o'clock... It's all a bit of a joke! Ha-Ha.'

It had not been quite such a joke as Laura made out. On her way to the opening the Rolls-Royce in which she was travelling was involved in an accident and she was thrown to the floor of the car. News of the collision reached the gallery and the BBC camera crew waiting to film her were beginning to pack up when her voice was heard through the doorway. She came in and carried on with the interview like the old trouper she was, a whisky in one hand and a cigarette in the other.

In fact the fall had given her a shock and for a while she could neither spell nor write, but the faculty came back; she was, as she said, a 'tough guy'. It was her last correspondence with Ella and she died a year later at Langford Place on 7 July 1970.

Ella sent Cornish cream to Miss Worth, Laura's secretary and companion in her last years, and cut out the obituaries. *The Times* had a long and rather critical column: 'her sympathy was not matched by an equal aesthetic appreciation'. (An attitude which persists today. Although she is well-known and her pictures command high prices, she still does not have the recognition she deserves as a major twentieth-century British artist.) The *Sunday Telegraph* described how her large circus picture in the *Queen Mary* now had pride of place in the reconstructed ship at Long Beach, California. The *Daily Telegraph* gave an account of the memorial service at St James's, Piccadilly. Ella also cut out an article about the forthcoming biography of Dame Laura Knight by Janet Dunbar, hinting at some surprising revelations. When the book was published the jacket design reproduced *Self and Nude*, bringing Laura and Ella together again though Ella was never to see it.

Ella collected the obituaries of her friends in an old envelope. Harold Knight had been the first, dying in 1961 at the age of eighty-seven at Colwall near Malvern where the Knights had lived since the war whilst keeping their London house. He had painted very little in his last years and had suffered from arthritis. The obituary in the *Telegraph* mentioned Laura more often than Harold; he had always lived in her shadow.

Dod Procter died in the summer of 1972 at Barncoose Hospital near Redruth. *The Times* recalled the sensation created by her painting *Morning* in 1927, when the public flocked to see the picture and the *Daily Mail* bought it for the nation. Alethea Garstin wrote an appreciation in the *Cornishman*: 'Distinguished, fastidious and dedicated to her work, Dod Procter's impeccable taste was evident in anything and everything with which she surrounded herself. Whether of little, great or no intrinsic value, each object was personal to her outstanding sense of fitness and beauty.' Along with her love of garden plants, these qualities belong to many of her contemporary women artists and Alethea Garstin's words could apply equally to herself, Gertrude Harvey or Ella Naper.

Other friends had passed away without obituaries in national papers. As early as 1943 Houghton Birch had become seriously ill. Ella informed Laura who wrote from the British Camp Hotel, Malvern: 'Poor John and Mornie – what a dreadful time they are having to say nothing of what poor Mouse is having to suffer. I hope she will not have to bear it long.'

Houghton died in June 1944 and Pog Yglesias made a terracotta relief for her gravestone in Paul cemetery. Bertie Hughes died in 1952, Lamorna Birch in 1955, Eleanor Hughes in 1959, Ruth Simpson in 1964. Gert Harvey, who had bathed naked with Ella and Laura in a pool of the Fowey river, wrote to say she was crawling around on one stick at Maen Cottage. She went into a nursing home at St Just where there were '15 invalids hidden away about the house' and where she had a nice room-mate in a wheelchair, though later she had a small room to herself. She died there in 1966. Charles Simpson died in 1971.

Ella was now in her eighties. Her great-niece Stella was only six or seven but she has a clear child's-eye picture of her great-aunt: frail, neat, elegant, wearing russet-coloured tweeds. With her weathered wrinkled face and slight frame she seemed very fragile. Maryella and her four daughters stayed at a nearby bed and breakfast; when the girls visited Ella at Trewoofe they had to be very quiet and take care not to break anything. The young child got the impression that Fleur the Pekinese ruled the roost. She remembers the smell of the house and how it was very still: the calico curtains, the blue and white Cornish crockery, vases of dried flowers, orange and gold.

Most of the garden was let to Willy Clemens who grew potatoes, onions and runner beans. Ella retained a small patch close to the house and terrace. Mary and Dennis Scobey kept an eye on her and friends visited: Mornie Kerr, Lamorna Birch's daughter from Flagstaff Cottage and Joan Evans, Gilbert Evans's widow from Oakhill. Valerie Powell had recently qualified as a nurse in London, and wanting a change of scene took a summer job with Rowena Cade at the Minack Theatre. At the end of the season she decided to stay on in Cornwall, finding work at the Edward Hain hospital, St Ives. All available accommodation was for winter lets and she required a permanent home; Dofferty sent her to Ella.

It was an ideal arrangement. The eighty-year-old and the twenty-year-old got on well together, leading separate lives and sharing the kitchen at different times. Ella retained the independence which meant so much to her but was not alone at night. Valerie remembers her as very frail with delicate bird-like bones but remarkably spirited. She remembers her sense of colour, the woodwork painted 'Naper blue', the paintings and ceramic figures, the flower beds outside the windows with primroses and grape hyacinths and later in the year marigolds. There was a lemon balm bush by the door; Ella used the leaves to scent the pillows for a good night's sleep. Valerie spent her days off at the Minack but they would have a chat when she returned. She understood how special Dozmary had been for Ella, a place where she and her friends relaxed away from the censorship of the village.

When Valerie went to Truro on a midwifery course she could only return occasionally. Irene Wellington, whose husband Hubert had died a year before Charlie, came down to be there, so that Ella could remain in her own home. Ella had no fear of dying; she saw it as part of nature and had no regrets. On the morning of 9 August 1972 Valerie came back from Truro and saw that Ella was very unwell; she called the doctor, who came and went. Ella died early in the afternoon, quietly and peacefully with Irene and Valerie in the room.

Her ashes were buried in the garden at Trewoofe next to Charlie's, close by the pond.

Index